CONTENTS

DUE BY

YORK NOTES

Measure for Measure

William Shakespeare

Notes by Emma Smith

Longman   York Press

The right of Emma Smith to be identified as Author of this Work has been asserted by her in accordance with the Copyright, Designs and Patents Act 1988

Exterior picture of the Globe Theatre reproduced by permission of the Raymond Mander and Joe Mitchenson Theatre Collection
Reconstruction of the Globe Theatre interior reprinted from Hodges: *The Globe Restored* (1968) by permission of Oxford University Press

YORK PRESS
322 Old Brompton Road, London SW5 9JH

ADDISON WESLEY LONGMAN LIMITED
Edinburgh Gate, Harlow,
Essex CM20 2JE, United Kingdom
Associated companies, branches and representatives throughout the world

First published 1999

ISBN 0-582-41464-4

Designed by Vicki Pacey, Trojan Horse, London
Phototypeset by Gem Graphics, Trenance, Mawgan Porth, Cornwall
Colour reproduction and film output by Spectrum Colour
Produced by Addison Wesley Longman China Limited, Hong Kong

PART ONE

INTRODUCTION

HOW TO STUDY A PLAY

Studying on your own requires self-discipline and a carefully thought-out work plan in order to be effective.

- Drama is a special kind of writing (the technical term is 'genre') because it needs a performance in the theatre to arrive at a full interpretation of its meaning. Try to imagine that you are a member of the audience when reading the play. Think about how it could be presented on the stage, not just about the words on the page.

- Drama is often about conflict of some sort (which may be below the surface). Identify the conflicts in the play and you will be close to identifying the large ideas or themes which bind all the parts together.

- Make careful notes on themes, character, plot and any subplots of the play.

- Why do you like or dislike the characters in the play? How do your feelings towards them develop and change?

- Playwrights find non-realistic ways of allowing an audience to see into the minds and motives of their characters, for example soliloquy, aside or music. Consider how such dramatic devices are used in the play.

- Think of the playwright writing the play. Why were these particular arrangements of events, characters and speeches chosen?

- Cite exact sources for all quotations, whether from the text itself or from critical commentaries. Wherever possible find your own examples from the play to back up your own opinions.

- Always express your ideas in your own words.

This York Note offers an introduction to *Measure for Measure* and cannot substitute for close reading of the text and the study of secondary sources.

Is it right to sleep with someone in return for a favour? Is a woman's virginity worth more than a man's life? Should prostitution be punished? Are those in power who preach about sexual morality hypocrites? Should society punish a man for getting his girlfriend pregnant? Is there a place for mercy in the legal system? Should we be interested in the private morality of public figures? Can the punishment ever fit the crime? Put like this, the questions asked by *Measure for Measure* are revealed to be strikingly modern: no wonder recent productions have dressed Angelo in a pinstripe suit and peopled Shakespeare's Vienna with the petty criminals and prostitutes of a modern-day urban underworld. In this play, Shakespeare puts morality and the law itself on trial, but the verdict can only be delivered by the audience. Of all Shakespeare's plays, it is the one which is most insistently full of questions, and which most clearly represents the grey areas which make up individual and social morality, now as well as in seventeenth-century England. Shakespeare's picture of urban life is darkly comic, as the play explores the intersections between different moral codes and standards while refusing ultimately to endorse any single viewpoint over another. The more you read or watch the play the more complicated and the more rewarding its ambiguities become.

Measure for Measure, then, is heavy on questions and correspondingly light on answers. Its characters and their actions and belief systems can be interpreted in more than one way: like those optical illusions that show a picture which, viewed one way is a rabbit and another a duck, it all depends how you look. Is Isabella heartless and selfish, or is she steadfastly true to a higher calling? Are the Duke's motives benevolent or sinister? Is Angelo a good man who is tempted or a hypocrite who preaches abstinence while craving indulgence? Do the play's final marriages symbolise social harmony or authoritarian control? Many of these choices, and others like them, become clearer through performance, and this note will refer to the play in the theatre wherever this offers a useful perspective. *Measure for Measure*'s predominant mode is one of questioning – we might call it interrogative – a play which forces us to think about the issues it presents and to supplement it with our own moral code. It is rather like a theatrical version of the game 'Scruples', in which players are confronted with a moral dilemma and must defend their own judgement to the others.

When Shakespeare's works were first gathered together for publication in the **First Folio** text of 1623, *Measure for Measure* was included among the comedies. Many readers have found this generic attribution inappropriate to this dark and complex play, preferring to see comedies as lightweight and frothy, concerned with love and romance rather than commercial sex and judicial punishment. At the end of the nineteenth century, the critic F.S. Boas dubbed *Measure for Measure*, along with *All's Well that Ends Well, Troilus and Cressida* and *Hamlet*, as a 'problem play', meaning that all four plays have as their core a moral or philosophical problem which the action is trying to resolve. But however useful it may be to highlight the problem of *Measure for Measure* – although it might be more difficult to isolate just a single problem – it is important not to forget its close fit with many of the features of Shakespearean comedy. The Jacobean playwright Thomas Heywood gives a contemporary view of a simple difference between comedy and tragedy: 'comedies begin in trouble and end in peace; tragedies begin in calms and end in tempest'. *Measure for Measure* certainly begins 'in trouble' – the Duke's abdication – but it is less clear that its conclusion, stage-managed by the Duke, represents the restoration of peace. Comedies feature the courtship of pairs of lovers, ending with their marriage, typically, sex itself is sublimated into the language of wooing, and we leave the main characters, as it were, at the bedroom door. In ending with marriages, *Measure for Measure* fulfils one of the common features of Shakespearean comedy as exemplified in *As You Like It* or *A Midsummer Night's Dream*, but in allowing, even depending on sex before marriage, *Measure for Measure* has disrupted the usual order of events. Even its marriages raise more questions than they offer solutions. Can Angelo and Mariana be happy, given the betrayal and deception which has engineered their union? Does Isabella, who is deafeningly silent in response to the Duke's proposal, accept her sudden lover, and if so, why doesn't she speak?

The fact that Shakespeare's plays are still studied and performed today may encourage us to think of them as timeless or perennial, rather than as specific to the culture and historical period of their composition. Looking at their immediate context can, however, offer insights into their concerns and interests. *Measure for Measure* was first performed at the court of the new king of England, James I, in 1604. The play is set in a city rife with problems of public morality – much like the way in which many contemporaries saw their own city, London. There are parallels between Shakespeare's Vienna and the London of the early seventeenth century, and, for the play's first audiences who were extremely clued in to topical references in the drama, there may be covert parallels between the Duke and James himself. It is this combination of sex, politics and the law which gives the play its tabloid *frisson* and its insistent moral equivocation, and which makes studying *Measure for Measure* so engaging and rewarding.

PART TWO

SUMMARIES & COMMENTARIES

On 26 December 1604, a play called 'Mesur for Mesur', written by 'Shaxberd' (in an age which had no standardised spelling, even proper names are written erratically, and even by their owners) was performed in the banqueting hall of the Palace of Whitehall in London. It is generally thought that the play was written earlier that same year, and that it may have been performed during the summer of 1604 in the public theatre. Some scholars have seen in Lucio's reference to the duke's 'composition with the King of Hungary' and the reply about 'peace' (I.2.1–4) an allusion to the peace negotiations between England and Spain which were taking place during the spring and summer of 1604, resulting in a peace declaration between the English sovereign and those of Spain and Austria in August. Another contemporary allusion may be uncovered in Pompey's announcement of a 'proclamation': 'All houses [brothels] in the suburbs of Vienna must be plucked down' (I.2.94–6). In September 1603 a law was proclaimed in London which allowed for the demolition of houses in the suburbs – where most brothels were located – in an attempt to stop the spread of Plague, and this order was enforced during the following months.

The play was first published in 1623, eight years after Shakespeare's (or Shaxberd's) death, in the First Folio edition of 'Mr William Shakespeares Comedies Tragedies & Histories'. It was listed under 'comedies' on the contents page, and its title is given with added punctuation as *Measure, for measure*. All modern editions, therefore, including J.M. Nosworthy's New Penguin Shakespeare edition to which this Note will refer, take this text as their basis. *Measure for Measure* is unusual in having a list of *dramatis personae* – 'The names of all the Actors' – and clearly defined location – 'The Scene Vienna' – appended to it in print. It is from this list of characters that the name of the Duke – Vincentio – and other details such as the description of Lucio as 'a fantastic' (someone who dresses or behaves eccentrically) and Escalus as 'an ancient Lord' are derived (see Background, on The Texts of Shakespeare's plays).

Measure for Measure is set in Vienna. The Duke Vincentio has decided to give up his authority and place it temporarily in the hands of his deputy, Angelo. Angelo is charged with bringing lapsed laws back into force and tackling the city's problems of prostitution and sex outside marriage. Instead of leaving Vienna as he claims, however, the Duke remains, disguised as a friar, to observe matters during his supposed absence.

One of the first acts of the new regime is the arrest of Claudio, whose girlfriend Juliet is pregnant. Claudio is condemned to death, despite his defence that the couple had a marital contract and were only waiting on certain practicalities to have an official ceremony. Claudio asks his friend Lucio to inform Isabella, his sister, who is about to enter a convent. Isabella goes to Angelo to plead for her brother's life, and the austere deputy finds himself sexually attracted to her. At their second meeting he offers to spare Claudio if she agrees to have sex with him. Isabella is horrified, refuses, and goes to tell her brother. In this interview, Claudio attempts to persuade her to go along with Angelo's proposal, voicing his own fear of death. Isabella refuses. The disguised Duke tells Claudio to prepare himself for death, and tells Isabella of a way to resolve the situation. Angelo's jilted sweetheart, Mariana, will go in place of Isabella to the assignation so that, having consummated their relationship, Angelo will be forced into marrying her. The pair go to Mariana, she agrees to this plan, and meets her former fiancé under cover of darkness.

The next day Angelo orders that Claudio be executed. The Duke arranges that another prisoner be executed instead of Claudio, but Barnadine refuses to be hanged, so the head of Ragozine, a prisoner who has died, is substituted. Isabella is told by the Duke that Claudio is dead. The Duke makes preparations for his return to office, and arranges a public meeting with his deputy. Isabella accuses Angelo, Mariana claims him as her lawful husband, and the Duke reveals that he has been privy to Angelo's deeds during his supposed absence. The Duke threatens to execute Angelo as recompense for his execution of Claudio, but Mariana persuades Isabella to plead for her husband. Claudio is revealed to be alive, and the Duke proposes marriage to Isabella.

ACT I

Duke Vincentio expresses his intention to leave Vienna for a time and to appoint a deputy to take his place. He invests his authority in Angelo, with Escalus as his second-in-command, and makes his departure

The play opens with the Duke addressing one of his lords, Escalus, and noting his familiarity with the laws and governance of Vienna. The Duke sends for Angelo, telling Escalus that he has chosen Angelo to serve as deputy during his absence. He asks Escalus's opinion of this choice, and Escalus agrees that 'if any in Vienna be of worth / To undergo such ample grace and honour / It is Lord Angelo' (lines 22–4). Angelo enters and the Duke bestows on him his authority, appointing Escalus as his 'secondary' (line 46). Angelo protests that some test of his worth should be made before giving him such responsibility, but the Duke assures him of his choice. The Duke seems in a hurry to depart and wants to slip away without a public fuss. He tells Angelo that his powers in government are exactly those of the Duke himself, promises to write to them about his news, and leaves. There is no information about where, or why, he is going. Escalus asks Angelo about his role in the new order, and Angelo promises to discuss it with him.

The scene raises many questions. Why is the Duke so eager to leave? Where is he going? How long does he intend to be away? Why has he chosen Angelo to be his deputy? Why did he not choose Escalus, after describing him as knowledgeable and experienced in matters of government? In performance Escalus has sometimes been shown anticipating that he will be appointed during the Duke's speech up to about line 15, when the truth of his plans begins to dawn. Is the Duke, as some critics of the play have claimed, setting a test for Angelo? Does he already have suspicions of him? We are introduced to two of the major players in the drama, the Duke and Angelo. The Duke's purposes and motives seem mysterious here. His language is often oblique and its **syntax** knotted: take his first lines 'Of government the properties to unfold / Would seem in me t'affect speech and discourse' (lines 3–4) which is a contorted way of beginning to say that he does not need to tell Escalus about the properties of government. Perhaps this is a sign of psychological or emotional stress (see

Characterisation). He expresses a desire for seclusion and a retreat from public life in his admission 'I love the people / But do not like to stage me to their eyes' (lines 67–8).

Angelo speaks only five times. He expresses himself the loyal servant of the Duke attending him in prompt answer to his summons; he asks for some further test of his mettle before the bestowal of such a duty; he offers to make some ceremony of the Duke's journey; he wishes blessings on his ruler's absence; and he promises to discuss Escalus's position with him. There are few clues to his character here. He does not question the Duke's decision except to offer his unworthiness, nor does he express surprise, pleasure, apprehension, humility, or any other emotion on hearing of this great change in his position. Loyalty, piety, and above all self-restraint, seem the keynotes of his responses.

4 **lists** bounds

11 **pregnant** knowledgeable

14 **warp** deviate

17 **with special soul** with complete conviction

20 **organs** instruments

29 **belongings** abilities

30 **proper** exclusively

36–40 **Nature never ... and use** Nature is like a creditor (one who is owed money) who never lends without stating how the loan should be used

41 **advertise** instruct

46 **secondary** deputy

48 **metal** (pun) metal/'mettle' – the imagery of stamping is from coin or medal minting

51 **leavened** considered

54 **prefers** presents

61 **something on** part of

70 **aves** commendations

78 **bottom of my place** basis of my duties

SCENE 2 Evidence of the tone of Angelo's new regime is presented: all brothels are to be pulled down and Claudio is imprisoned awaiting execution for getting Juliet pregnant outside marriage. Claudio asks Lucio to contact his sister to get her to plead with Angelo for his life

Lucio is engaged in some bawdy jesting with two gentlemen when they are joined by the brothel-keeper Mistress Overdone. They continue to joke about venereal diseases and their familiarity with her house until she tells them about Claudio, who is 'worth five thousand of you all' (lines 60–1) but who has been taken to prison. In three days he will be executed for getting Juliet pregnant. The men go off to investigate this rumour. Pompey, Mistress Overdone's servant, enters, as a gaoler and another hapless prisoner cross the stage. His offence, Pompey announces, is, like Claudio's: fornication. Pompey tells Mistress Overdone that there has been an order that all brothels are to be pulled down, and she fears for her livelihood. Pompey urges her to change her trade to innkeeper, and he will serve as her tapster. Claudio enters, under arrest, along with Juliet. His gaoler tells him that he is acting on Angelo's authority. When Lucio asks Claudio what has happened, Claudio talks of excessive liberty which has brought about restraint. He tells Lucio that he and Juliet were betrothed and that she is his wife in all but name: 'She is fast my wife / Save that we do denunciation lack / Of outward order' (lines 146–8). They were waiting only for the settlement of her dowry before proceeding to a formal marriage ceremony. Claudio attributes his arrest to the zeal of the city's new ruler. Whereas before, under the Duke, the law was neglected for 'nineteen zodiacs' (line 167), now Angelo is treating the city as a rider on an unfamiliar horse who 'lets it straight feel the spur' (line 161) so as to establish his authority over the beast. Lucio suggests that they send after the Duke to seek his intervention in the case, but Claudio asserts that he is 'not to be found' (line 174). Instead he urges Lucio to find his sister, about to enter into a convent, and implore her to intercede with Angelo for mercy on his behalf. He expresses some confidence in her persuasive powers. Lucio promises to enact this commission.

The scene shifts from joking about prostitution and politics to their harsh realities as Angelo's new regime begins to bite.

News of his plans to enforce laws more strictly reaches the community of reprobates who stand to lose by them. The speeches of Lucio, the gentlemen, Pompey and Mistress Overdone are all in prose, giving a freer, more earthy tone to the first part of the scene. This changes abruptly with the entrance of the captive Claudio at line 115. His **blank verse** speeches may signify his worth – Shakespeare often uses prose for lower-rank or comic characters – thereby distinguishing him from the other characters in the scene. This distinction is particularly obvious in the contrast between the speeches of Claudio and Lucio: where Claudio speaks the measured, educated and philosophical **iambic pentameters** of lines 124–9 or 144–54, Lucio responds in inappropriately chirpy and irreverent prose, making a joke of one who can 'speak so wisely under an arrest' (line 130) and offering the comfortless observation that 'thy head stands so tickle on thy shoulders' (line 171). His demeanour throughout the scene is jesting, even satirical. By contrast, Claudio is established as serious and sober, not the good-for-nothing we might expect from the description of his crimes before his entrance. When he gives his side of the story, however, his assertion that he and Juliet were betrothed, having entered into a marriage contract, mitigates the severity of his actions and renders the authority's responses all the more extreme. His assessment of Angelo's actions as the new governor of Vienna is astute (lines 156–69). The theme of antithesis is established in his analysis of too much freedom leading to control: 'every scope by the immoderate use / Turns to restraint' (lines 126–7) (see Themes – Symmetry & Antithesis; Freedom & Restraint).

2 **composition** agreement

11 **razed** erased

22 **proportion** verse metre

29 **lists** selvages, edges of fabric such as velvet

32 **three-piled piece** expensive, triple-ply velvet

33 **lief** rather

kersey coarse woven cloth

piled of fabric, but also punning on haemorrhoids and baldness as symptoms of syphilis

34 **French velvet** expensive imported fabric, but also punning on 'French' = venereal disease

43 **tainted** infected

free free from disease

49 **dolours** pains, with a pun on 'dollars', currency

51 **French crown** money, but punning on the baldness caused by syphilis

82 **sweat** sweating sickness, or Plague

83 **custom-shrunk** short of trade

92 **maid** small fish (with a pun on trouts, line 89)

95 **houses** bawdy houses, brothels

108 **tapster** barman

113 **provost** official who oversees executions

128 **ravin** devour

bane poison

132 **foppery** foolishness

146 **She is fast my wife** they have pledged themselves by hand-fasting or betrothal

147 **denunciation** public proclamation

149 **propagation** increasing

151 **meet** best, proper

171 **an** if

tickle precarious

177 **approbation** probation

182 **prone** apt

dialect language of argument

189 **tick-tack** game involving knocking pegs into holes, hence an obvious sexual reference

SCENE 3   The Duke meets Friar Thomas and explains the reasons for his retirement from office, citing the laxity into which the laws have fallen and the need for a new authority to implement their reinforcement. He also indicates his intention to remain in Vienna disguised as a friar

The scene opens on a conversation between the Duke and a friar, and the Duke's first words seem to be denying that it is love which has caused him to abdicate his ducal responsibilities. The Duke tells the friar, whom he clearly knows well ('none knows better than you' – line 8) that he prefers a secluded life, and also that the laws of Vienna have fallen into disuse and are not respected. He has appointed Angelo, a 'man of stricture and firm abstinence' (line 12) in his place. The friar suggests that it would have been more imposing for the Duke himself to have applied the lapsed laws with more severity, but the Duke replies that having presided over their decline this new course would be a 'tyranny' (line 36). Rather he is going to entrust it to Angelo while remaining in Vienna in the guise of a friar to 'behold his sway' (line 43). He requests a habit and tuition in friar-like behaviour. The last lines of the scene seem to express some suspicion about how Angelo will bear his commission: 'Hence shall we see, / If power change purpose, what our seemers be.'

The main purpose of this scene is to add to our knowledge about the Duke. Friar Thomas's interjections serve only to prompt the Duke to tell us some of what we want to know and answer some of the questions aroused by the Duke's conduct in I.1. The Duke begins, however, in terms which seem designed to prolong the speculation about his actions and motives rather than end it. He has a 'purpose / More grave and wrinkled than the aims and ends / Of burning youth' (lines 4–6). In fact his 'purpose' seems more plural than singular: three justifications for his retirement from office are given in the scene, without any acknowledgement that this triplication makes his departure at once overdetermined (there are more reasons for an action than are strictly necessary) and yet still mysterious. The Duke even offers further reasons 'at our more leisure' (line 49). First the Duke reminds the friar, and the audience, of a character trait suggested in I.1.67–70, that of a personal desire for seclusion: 'I have ever loved the life removed' (line 8). Next, he discusses the way the law has fallen into disuse, echoing Claudio's analysis a few minutes earlier in lines 164–70 of the previous scene – although there is some disagreement over the length of this lapse, measured by Claudio at 'nineteen zodiacs' (I.2.167) and by the Duke at 'fourteen years' (line 21) (see Treatment of Time). The friar's suggestion that the Duke himself would have had greater authority to 'unloose this tied-up justice' (line 32) also questions the logic of this factor as a legitimate reason for the Duke's withdrawal from rule. Thirdly, the Duke seems to have an ulterior motive, that of testing Angelo and observing whether his character is corrupted by power and whether he is truly as he seems. The fact that this last reason is emphatically placed at the end of the scene gives it added weight, and begins to flesh out earlier suggestions of a manipulative, even **Machiavellian**, side to his character (see Textual Analysis, Text 1).

2 **dribbling** from archery, referring to an arrow which falls wide of the mark

3 **complete** impenetrable

12 **stricture** strictness

20 **bits** part of a bridle held in the horse's mouth

35 **Sith** since

SCENE 4 **Isabella is discussing her imminent entry into the convent with one of the nuns. She expresses her wish for stricter rules. Lucio arrives to tell her of her brother Claudio's imprisonment and of his wish that she should plead with Angelo on his behalf. She agrees to try**

In conversation with the nun, Isabella asks about any 'farther privileges' (line 1) allowed to members of the order. The nun misunderstands and thinks she is keen for more freedom, whereas what Isabella wants is 'a more strict restraint' (line 4). This interchange is interrupted, however, by Lucio, who brings the news of Claudio's arrest. Isabella's response to the news that Juliet – whom she has known since their childhood – is pregnant is that the couple should marry. Lucio tells that this course of action is impossible under Angelo's government, describing his aversion to sensuality as an almost inhuman coldness, one whose blood is 'snow-broth' (line 58). He urges her to petition Angelo for a pardon for her brother. She is hesitant about her abilities, but is persuaded to try.

In giving us our first sight of Isabella, this scene completes Act I's series of introductions. From her first appearance on the stage, Isabella is associated with her religious vocation. She seems on the brink of joining the order when Lucio arrives, and throughout the rest of the play we never see her return to the convent. While her initial speech requests more restraint in the order of St Clare, her subsequent responses to Lucio's news show that she is not immune to worldly concerns. She is not shocked or judgemental about Juliet's pregnancy or her brother's culpability, but she is profoundly affected by the thought of Claudio's punishment. Her speeches become short, cropped lines expressive of her emotional response to the news. While she doubts her powers to affect Angelo, she resolves to do what she can, displaying a decisive practicality at odds with many stereotypical impressions of nuns. Lucio is eloquent in the scene, and through comparison with his previous appearance in I.2, it is possible to see his role as go-between emerging (see Characterisation). Also in comparison with I.2 it is noticeable that here he uses verse not prose, perhaps modulating his speech to the more austere atmosphere of the cloisters. His language is often unexpectedly poetic, as in his description on Isabella as 'a thing enskied and sainted' (line 34) and in the fruitful imagery of natural fertility used to describe Claudio and Juliet's relationship (lines 40–4). He also adds to the sense of mystery about the Duke in his remark that 'his givings-out [pronouncements] were of an infinite distance / From his true-meant design' (lines 54–5).

5 **Saint Clare** a religious order founded by St Clare and St Francis of Assisi in 1212 which imposed strict restrictions on its members who lived a life of poverty, charity and devotion

17 **stead** help

25 **weary** long-winded

32 **lapwing** in *Much Ado About Nothing* (III.1.24) Shakespeare seems to associate the lapwing with frivolous prattling

42 **seedness** sown seeds

43 **foison** harvest

49 **tilth** arable land

60 **rebate** make dull

70 **pith** purpose

72 **censured** condemned

86 **Mother** prioress

87 **affair** business

ACT II

SCENE 1 Escalus tries to suggest leniency towards Claudio but Angelo will hear none of it, and orders Claudio's execution for the next morning. Elbow the constable brings before them the garbled case of immorality against Pompey and Froth. Angelo impatiently leaves the matter to Escalus who dismisses them with a warning to reform

At the opening of the scene, Angelo and Escalus each talk about their view of the law. Angelo takes a hard line: the law must not be made a 'scarecrow' (line 1). Escalus tries to argue for Claudio as part of a good family, and suggests that even Angelo, 'most strait in virtue' (line 9), must recognise the force of temptation and therefore be merciful. Angelo admits the point about temptation but argues that the law is not discredited simply because those involved with it are not themselves perfect. Instead of pardoning the prisoner because his faults are so familiar, the judge who behaves likewise should himself be punished. Escalus does not argue further, and Angelo despatches the Provost with the warrant for Claudio's execution the next day. The austerity of this interchange is dispersed by the entry of Elbow the constable with two prisoners, Pompey and Froth. Elbow's unintelligible deposition uses many words wrongly (**malapropisms**) thus making a mockery of the scene. Pompey's speeches of self-defence are similarly digressive as he spins out Elbow's story and makes a counteraccusation about the character of Elbow's wife. Angelo gives up the courtroom in exasperation, and leaves Escalus in charge 'Hoping you'll find good cause to whip them all' (line 131). Escalus dismisses Froth and talks to Pompey, asking him about his business. Pompey's responses are irreverent but pragmatic, arguing that if prostitution is to be banned, then it will be necessary to 'geld and splay all the youth of the city' (lines 219–20). He is dismissed with a warning which he shows no signs of heeding. Escalus suggests that other local citizens might be found to take the burden of the office of constable from Elbow, and then invites the Justice, who has been silent since the beginning of the scene, home to dine with him. The Justice states simply that 'Lord Angelo is severe' (line 269), and Escalus makes an attempt to defend his superior's actions, but the scene ends with his mournful recognition that 'there is no remedy' for 'poor Claudio' (line 272).

It would be easy to see this scene as a long comic sequence sandwiched between two more serious and significant sections and to dismiss the buffoonery of Elbow and Pompey to focus on Escalus and Angelo. There is, however, more coherence in the themes, if not the tone, of the scene than this description suggests. As often in Shakespeare's plays, comic characters revisit or rework themes and issues in the subplot to amplify their more 'serious' presentation elsewhere. Here in *Measure for Measure*, the central theme of the operation of justice and the law is considered on different levels and through different scenarios, as in this particular scene. The opening exchange between Escalus and Angelo offers an important insight into Angelo's behaviour. We have not seen him on stage since his few words in the first scene, although he has been mentioned in every intervening scene. His opening words 'we must not' establish his unbending fixity of opinion, and his mention of the 'terror' (line 4) shows how thoroughly he has assumed the role set out by the Duke, who uses the same word in I.1 19 and I.3.26. In using an image of animals to refer to the populace he could be seen to demonstrate a lack of human concern for the people. He is unaffected by Escalus's arguments for clemency, turning them round to support firmer punishments rather than leniency. He does, however, allow for the possibility of temptation, recognising that a member of the jury may be more guilty than the prisoner he is trying, or anyone would pick up and keep a jewel which if he had not seen he would not have been tempted by. His harshness, however, is represented as entirely consistent: he would wish for the same punishment on himself were he guilty as others. He asserts firmly, coldly, that 'he must die', and urges the Provost to arrange for Claudio to see his confessor before death. Escalus's speech beginning 'Well, heaven forgive him' (lines 37–40) has a curiously sententious, or moralising, tone which generalises from the particular situation. It is end-rhymed which may make it sound more proverbial, and it is not clear how it relates to the foregoing conversation. The irruption of Elbow and his prisoners into the scene introduces another tone, that of prose comedy. Elbow's confusion of words – 'benefactors' instead of 'malefactors', 'cardinally' for 'carnally' etc. – and Pompey's obfuscation give an ironic and comic twist to the earlier exchanges about justice and punishment. In place of the language of morality and desert invoked by Angelo and Escalus, Pompey presents his own, more practical and pragmatic code of behaviour as he summarises in his exit-line: 'I thank your worship for your good counsel; but I shall follow it as the flesh and fortune shall better determine' (lines 240–2). Pompey speaks the language of moral expediency in the knowledge that laws do not change human behaviour nor cure human weakness. Amid all this side-tracking wordplay, the law looks like an ass in this scene: Angelo leaves in exasperation and the symbolically named figure of Justice is pointedly silent until the very last lines, when it is Angelo, not the 'benefactors', on whom he delivers a verdict (see Themes, on Crime, Punishment & Justice).

2 **fear** scare away

5 **keen** sharp-edged

most strait rigorous, strict

12–13 **Or that ... purpose** if you could have acted decisively to have sex

19 **passing** passing sentence

23 **pregnant** obvious, full of meaning

30 **pattern out** be an example for

36 **pilgrimage** lifespan

39 **brakes** thickets

56 **comes off well** is well delivered

57 **quality** rank, status, or occupation

59 **out at elbow** (proverbial phrase) worn out, as of old clothes

61 **parcel** part-time

64 **hot-house** bath-house, but such places had a dubious reputation, hence a secondary meaning of brothel

66 **detest** Pompey's mistake for 'protest'

77 **cardinally** misused for 'carnally'

85 **misplaces** misuses words

87 **stewed prunes** commonly associated with prostitution and brothels

113 **Come me to** get to the point

119 **Hallowmas** All Saints' (or Hallows') Day, 1 November

120 **Allhallond Eve** Hallowe'en, or 31 October

122 **lower chair** unknown, but perhaps referring to an easy chair or couch

125 **open** public

154 **an it like you** if it please you

respected misused for 'suspected'

164 **Justice or Iniquity** ironic personifications attached to Elbow and Pompey, and which may refer to stock characters from medieval morality plays

166 **caitiff** villain

167 **Hannibal** misused for 'cannibal'

171 **battery** assault, but misused for 'slander' as Escalus observes

179 **courses** way of life

190 **Overdone** given the name of Overdone, but with a suggestion of sexual exhaustion

199 **taphouse** tavern

208 **Pompey the Great** Roman general defeated by Julius Caesar

219 **geld and splay** castrate and spay or sterilise

223 **take order** make arrangements

drabs prostitutes

226 **heading** beheading

230 **three pence a bay** a ridiculously low rent, used by Pompey as a measure of unlikelihood

237 **shrewd** harsh

243 **carman** cart or wagon drive

256 **jade** inferior horse

wit intelligence

258 **go through with all** perform all the duties

260 **sufficient** able

264 **Eleven** perhaps symbolic – the eleventh hour is just in time (see Matthew 20:1–16)

SCENE *2*   **Encouraged by Lucio, Isabella visits Angelo to plead for Claudio's life. Angelo will not yield and asserts the justice of his sentence. Angelo wavers and tells her to return the next day. After she has left, he reflects on how she has aroused his lust**

The scene begins with an exchange between Angelo and the Provost, in which the order of execution on Claudio is reiterated. The Provost tries to suggest that Angelo may repent of this command when it is too late but Angelo is unbending and threatens to appoint a new provost if he is not obeyed. Angelo also arranges for Juliet, 'the fornicatress', to be given 'needful, but not lavish, means' (lines 23–4). Isabella and Lucio are admitted. Isabella begins, somewhat hesitantly, to explain her purpose, pleading with Angelo for leniency. When Angelo repeats his firm views, she seems ready to give in – 'O just, but severe law' (line 41), but Lucio urges her to try harder, telling her she is too 'cold' (line 45) in her pleas. She sets to her task of persuasion again with more passion, but Angelo is adamant, arguing that the law 'hath slept' (line 90) but 'now 'tis awake' (line 93) and must therefore be enforced with due severity. As Isabella's oratory becomes more ardent, Lucio and the Provost suggest that her words are having some effect on their hearer, and finally Angelo relents from his absolute position and tells her to return the next day. An **aside** gives an indication of his motives: 'I am that way going to temptation. / Where prayers cross' (lines 158–9). His **soliloquy** expands on this theme, as Angelo muses on his previous immunity to sexual desire and the sudden longings Isabella has provoked in him. For the first time, he understands the vulnerability engendered by desire.

This is an electrifying scene in which two of the play's principals meet and the dynamic between them sets the subsequent action in motion (see Textual Analysis, Text 2). It is Angelo's third appearance and, throughout the play so far, adjectives such as 'severe' (II.1.269), 'strait in virtue' (II.1.9) and 'precise' (I.3.50) have been attached to him. The Duke's suggestion at the end of I.4 that perhaps this upright, uptight ruler is not all he seems has, however, set up the expectation of Angelo's fall. Here we see it beginning. At the opening of the scene Angelo is all certainty and resolution, signing papers, giving orders, dispensing commands with no thought for the human consequences. At Isabella's entrance, his certainty starts to dissolve. As soon as he sees her he tells the Provost to stay with them – he seems to want more people at the interview. For a while he is able to maintain his own cold equanimity, reiterating arguments about punishment which we have heard in his conversation with Escalus in the previous scene: the answer to the high incidence of crime is not to be lenient but to be more strict, and the fact that the crimes may be those to which figures in authority are themselves susceptible does not mean that they should go unpunished. Isabella's arguments echo those of Escalus but her stress is on mercy as the pre-eminent quality of authority. Claudio, she says, would be merciful to Angelo were he guilty of the same crime (see Themes, on Substitution). (There is fine **dramatic irony** in the fact that Angelo will commit the same crime of premarital sex later in the play and that even here in this scene his thoughts are lustful.) Her language employs the religious terms 'grace' (lines 62, 78), 'mercy' (lines 50, 63), 'pity' (line 99), and she talks of the ultimate ruler, God, 'He, which is the top of judgement' (line 75). She even offers a 'bribe', using an earthly term to get Angelo's attention and then promising a spiritual, not material, bargain from the prayers of 'fasting maids' (line 154) and the rewards of heaven. Angelo's speeches stress the iniquity of sin and the punitive side of justice rather than its abstract properties, using words such as 'condemn' (lines 37–8), 'fault' (lines 39, 40), 'forfeit' (line 71), 'edict' (line 92), 'offence' (line 102), 'foul wrong' (line 103). For him the law is an absolute; Isabella appeals to a higher sense of justice.

When Angelo tells her 'your brother is a forfeit of the law' (line 71), a formulation which implicitly distinguishes himself from the criminal Claudio, she counters with the Christian idea that 'all the souls that were were forfeit once' (line 73) before being redeemed through God's mercy, thus demolishing any moral ground from which to judge another by asserting that the common inheritance of humanity is its sinfulness. Having been accused of coldness by Lucio she has warmed to her persuasive theme, moving from the specific case of Claudio to a rhetorical disquisition on human authority and its limitations and dominating the scene through her eloquence. Angelo is reduced to half-lines or to short, stiffly formal assertions of his position. Throughout this shift of power, there is considerable tension and energy between them (see Textual Analysis). Angelo's final soliloquy is the first time he is alone on stage and gives us an insight into his character (see Characterisation). The speech is choppy and full of rhetorical questions and broken phrases, expressing his attempt to come to terms with his unfamiliar and powerful response to Isabella. His lustful feelings run counter to his sense of his own identity, causing him to question his very self: the question 'What dost thou?' leads inexorably to 'what art thou?' (line 173) for a man who has built his whole sense of himself on his chastity and self-restraint. In seeing Angelo struggle with himself we may feel more sympathy for him as the form of the soliloquy allows us a particular access to his thoughts and emotions. The play rarely affords us such privileged insight into its other characters.

4 **He hath ... dream** Claudio has not offended in reality

10 **Under your good correction** correct me if I'm wrong

37 **let it be his fault** eliminate the fault rather than Claudio

40 **To fine** to punish

52 **Look what** whatever

59 **longs** belongs

74 **all the souls ... once** referring to existence before Christian redemption

79 **man new made** for Christians, God's forgiveness was like a second creation

85 **fowl of season** the bird at the best time for eating

95 **glass** mirror or globe, crystal ball in which the future is revealed

98 **successive degrees** further stages

111 **Jove** God of thunder

112 **pelting** insignificant

116 **unwedgeable** so strong it cannot be split by iron wedges

120 **glassy** various glosses have been proposed here, including brittle, transparent, or reflected in a mirror

122 **spleens** this organ was regarded as the seat of laughter

126 **We cannot ... ourself** there is no single scale of judgement, as there are different standards for those in authority from those for their inferiors

130 **choleric** angry

136 **skins** covers superficially, rather than healing

142 **sense** sensuality

149 **sicles** shekels, coins

150 **stones** jewels

159 **prayers cross** contradict each other, are at cross-purposes

166–8 **That lying ... season** under the sun the violet (Isabella) flourishes, while the carrion (Angelo) rots

172 **fie** expression of disgust or revulsion

180 **cunning enemy** the devil

185 **temper** mood

187 **fond** infatuated

SCENE 3   **The Duke, disguised as a friar, visits Juliet in prison and commends her for her repentance. He tells her of Claudio's fate**

The disguised Duke tells the Provost that he is making a charitable visit to the prisoners and gains access to Juliet. The Provost tells him that the father of her unborn baby is to be executed for the deed the next day. Juliet tells the Duke that she loves Claudio and that sex was 'mutually committed' (line 27) (see Sources), but she also expresses repentance. Hearing of Claudio's punishment she is horrified.

This short scene contrasts with the extended tension of the previous one, and sees the Duke's first entrance in disguise and Juliet's only words (she makes silent appearances in I.2 and V.1). The Duke hears of Angelo's severity in the punishment of Claudio, and he encourages Juliet to repent of her behaviour. His pious observations may suffer from the audience's knowledge that his friar's habit is a disguise rather than a genuine vocation. Juliet is repentant but cuts short the Duke's homily (line 34). In stressing the moral and religious aspect of Juliet's behaviour and her primary allegiance to a religious rather than social law, the Duke may seem to ally himself with Isabella's sense of justice rather than Angelo's.

12 **blistered her report** spoiled her reputation

21 **arraign** accuse

23 **hollowly** falsely

28 **heavier kind** whether women or men were seen to be most at fault in such matters is unclear; the Duke may be punning on 'heavier' as a description of Juliet's pregnancy

30 **meet** right

30–4 **lest you ... in fear** distinguishing between true repentance arising from love for God, and false repentance prompted by fear of divine punishment

39 ***Benedicite*** bless you

SCENE 4 **Angelo tells Isabella that he will spare Claudio if she agrees to have sex with him. She threatens to expose his hypocrisy but he taunts that no-one will believe her, and she admits the truth of this. She reflects that she cannot give up her virtue at any price**

Angelo's soliloquy meditates on his struggle between physical desire and self-restraint, and Isabella's appointed visit is announced. She is suppliant and it is for him to tell her his decision. He does this with some circumlocution, quibbling that her brother must die, in the sense that all people must die, but that his life might be extended. He comes to the point, offering her a choice between her brother's execution under 'most just law' (line 52) or her submission 'to such sweet uncleanness / As she that he [Claudio] hath stained' (lines 54–5). Isabella seems not to understand him, and continues to beg for Claudio's life. 'I'll speak more gross' (line 82), says Angelo, and reiterates his terms. Her response is fiery and adamant, and she asserts that her brother's swift death is preferable to the eternal damnation of the sin proposed by Angelo. Angelo notes that she seemed less condemnatory of the fault in Claudio but she argues that she only excused it for her greater love of her brother. When he tells her he loves her, Isabella retorts that for the same crime Claudio is condemned to death (see Themes, on Symmetry & Antithesis). She tries to regain the upper hand in the scene by threatening to 'tell the world / What man thou art' (lines 153–4). Angelo counters that no-one will believe such a report because of his unblotted reputation, and urges her again that her brother's death will be the result of her refusal to yield to his desires. He tells her to return the next day with her answer. In Isabella's final speech after he has left, she recognises that she has no hope of exposing his hypocrisy. She reflects that Claudio would never want her to agree to such a bargain for his sake because 'More than our brother is our chastity' (line 185). She resolves to visit him in prison and 'fit his mind to death' (line 187).

> Angelo's last appearance at the end of scene 2 was in soliloquy; this scene opens with another, giving the impression that he has been struggling with his desires ever since his first interview with Isabella. His speech is oblique and troubled: he states that his words of prayer are empty because 'his invention' (his thoughts)

'Anchors on Isabel' (line 4). Angelo's phrase 'false seeming' (line 15) anticipates Isabella's bitter denunciation 'Seeming, seeming!' (line 150): both echo the Duke's plan in I.3.54, 'what our seemers be', as the truth behind Angelo's seeming propriety has been revealed. Isabella's opening line is problematic. There is a definite, perhaps unwitting, sexual meaning in 'I am come to know your pleasure' (line 31), particularly as it follows Angelo's feverish account of the mounting lust in his blood, and many critics have commented on the imagery of sexual sado-masochism with which she rejects Angelo's proposition: 'Th'impression of keen whips I'd wear as rubies, / And strip myself to death as to a bed / That long I have been sick for' (lines 101–3) (see Characterisation). If Isabella's language is subconsciously sexual, however, she is slow to pick up on Angelo's overt approach. The scene is full of tense formulations of equivalence and exchange as both of them explore and assert their individual moral codes, and these can be imagined as oppositions: the soul v. the body, sin v. charity, swift death v. eternal damnation, Isabella's ignorance v. her sexual teasing. All these are versions of and elaborations on the central exchange of sex v. life (see Themes, on Symmetry & Antithesis; Substitution). No compromise or accommodation or negotiation is possible in this clashing of extreme and absolute choices.

Whereas in previous scenes it was Angelo who was always adamant and inflexible, here Isabella assumes that position. At their last interview she made the case for mercy amid the general unworthiness of humanity and here it is Angelo who asserts, as part justification, part recognition, 'We are all frail' (line 121). The scene escalates to a climax in his admission 'now I give my sensual race the rein' (line 160): his time for soul-searching and struggling against temptation is past as he becomes increasingly driven by his desires. Isabella's soliloquy – her only one in the play – expresses her reliance on Claudio's agreeing with her decision. The emotion of the preceding encounter has infused her speech with **hyperbole**: 'had he twenty heads to tender down' (line 180). She resolves on absolutes, delivered in the starkly precise and clipped diction of 'Then, Isabel, live chaste, and, brother, die' (line 185) and her last four lines fall into two **couplets** emphasising the finality of her moral decision.

3 **invention** thought

7 **conception** creation, intention

9 **seared** dried up

    gravity propriety, sober living

11 **boot** advantage

    idle plume foolish, frivolous feather worn in the hat

12 **place** position of authority

15 **Blood** sexual appetite

16–17 **Let's write … crest** the precise meaning of these lines is unclear, but they elaborate on Angelo's good / evil opposition between 'seeming' and being

19 **Teach** show

22 **dispossessing** depriving

27 **general** public

29 **untaught** ignorant

45 **saucy** lecherous

    coin God's image produce bastard children (the image is of counterfeit coins)

48 **restrainèd** forbidden

51 **pose** pose a problem

57–8 **Our compelled … accompt** referring to the proverb that 'compelled sins are no sins'

59 **warrant** endorse

61 **recorded law** written, pre-existing statutes

73 **nothing of your answer** not something for which you are responsible

75 **craftily** deceptively

79 **black masks** perhaps referring to the black veil worn by the order of St Clare

80 **enshield** defended

90 **in the loss of question** for the sake of argument

97 **supposed** imagined person

111 **Ignomy in ransom** freedom obtained at shameful price

112 **two houses** as of two different families, unrelated

115 **sliding** lapse

119 **something** somewhat

122 **fedary** confederate

123 **Owe and succeed** own and inherit

127–8 **Men their … by them** men degrade themselves as superior beings when they take advantage of women's frailty

130 **credulous to false prints** another image from counterfeiting, suggesting that women are easily moulded

134 **arrest** take you at

138 **destined livery** the costume of frailty which is the lot of womankind

147 **pluck on others** test others

151 **proclaim** denounce in public

156 **vouch** assertion

160 **I give my sensual race the rein** give free rein to my sexual inclinations

162 **nicety** coyness

prolixious superfluous

163 **banish what they sue for** are so alluring they heighten rather than appease the lover's desires

174 **approof** approval

178 **prompture** prompting

180 **tender down** lay down in payment

ACT III

SCENE 1   The friar/Duke urges Claudio to prepare himself for death. Isabella tells Claudio about Angelo's proposition, and while he is initially horrified, he tries to persuade her to do it to save his life. She leaves angrily. The Duke then tells Claudio that Angelo is only testing Isabella and there is no hope of a pardon. Claudio repents his treatment of his sister. The Duke unfolds to Isabella a plan to resolve the situation: Angelo's jilted sweetheart Mariana will take Isabella's place

At the beginning of the scene, Claudio professes himself 'prepared to die' (line 4), and the Duke, in his role as friar, delivers a long speech on the worthlessness of life and the folly of holding it so dear. All life is fear of death, he preaches, and therefore death should be sought as an early release from this servitude. Claudio repeats his sentiments of resignation to his fate. This is an important prelude to the encounter with Isabella, in which Claudio's stoicism is rapidly contradicted by his attempts to save his own life through his sister. Isabella enters and offers her brother the comfort of his imminent trip to heaven. In response to his asking whether there is any alternative, she admits that there is but that it is at a price too high. She explains Angelo's proposition, beginning to doubt her brother's response as she does so. He agrees that she should not sacrifice herself in this way. Gradually, however, the possibility of his escape dawns on him, and he begins to suggest that it would not be a sin to save his life. He speaks eloquently of the terrors of death, 'to die, and go we know not where, / To lie in cold obstruction and to rot' (lines 121–2) in contrast to his earlier resignation. Isabella is angry at his suggestion and leaves. The Duke intervenes to have some private conversation with her, first telling Claudio that he has heard Angelo's confession and knows that his proposal to Isabella is only a trick and that there is no hope of his sentence being lifted. He must prepare himself for death. Claudio wishes pardon from his sister for his behaviour. Then the Duke tells Isabella of his plan. Angelo had been engaged to marry a woman named Mariana, whose brother was drowned along with her dowry, before the wedding. Hearing that she had no riches to bring him, Angelo broke off the engagement under the guise of having heard some rumours about his fiancée's morality and character. Despite this cruelty, however, Mariana maintains her love for her erstwhile sweetheart. The Duke proposes that Isabella go along with Angelo's scheme and set a place for them to meet. There they will interpose Mariana in her place, and then put pressure on Angelo to marry her with the revelation that he has already slept with her. Isabella agrees with this plan.

> This long scene is packed with incident, revelation and emotion, all pivoting on the activities of the disguised Duke. In his sermon about the meaning of life delivered to Claudio, he urges him to 'Be absolute for death' (line 5), encouraging the hapless prisoner in the kind of absolute certainty and single-mindedness which has already been seen to motivate both Angelo and Isabella. The Duke's discourse uses many examples and images to persuade his listener of the futility of a life spent in the shadow of death. The language is

reductive, humans are merely 'death's fool' (line 11), consisting of 'many a thousand grains / That issue out of dust' (lines 20–1). The speech is crammed with negatives, with the repeated phrase 'thou art not' (lines 13, 19 and 23) echoed in 'Thou'rt by no means' (line 15), 'Thou hast not' (line 36), and 'Thou hast neither' (line 37). This catalogue of reasons why death is actually to be preferred over life stresses the burden of existence, in contrast to Claudio's subsequent speech in lines 121–35 which focuses, in panic and despair, on the fearful and unknown passage of death itself. The Duke's philosophy of stoicism is markedly unsuited to his friar's costume: where Christian religion might well preach the futility of life on earth, it does so with reference to the greater glories of the afterlife. There is no mention of judgement or life after death in the Duke's long speech, and because he delivers it from his disguised position, it is hard to know quite how to read it. For Roger Allam, who played the Duke in the 1987 production of the play by the Royal Shakespeare Company, this passage was crucial to his whole idea of his character: 'I found that if I related the lines to myself as much as to Claudio the speech was unlocked for me, and a central part of the Duke's character fell into place. His sense of self has fragmented into 'many a thousand grains' of dust …. In a sense the purpose of the Duke's journey through the play so far is to realise completely his own sceptical fatalism. But somehow this can only be expressed through someone else's situation' (see Critical History & Broader Perspectives; Characterisation). This argues that the Duke's words, so cheerless to the man who is staring death in the face, are revelatory about his own personality at this point in the play. The truth of the speech is, however, subtly distorted by the fact of the Duke's disguise and his wider, but as yet undelivered, plans that Claudio shall not in fact die and that therefore the question of his preparedness for death is irrelevant.

It is important that the Duke overhears Isabella's conversation with her brother, for it is here that news of Angelo's hypocrisy reaches him. Isabella and Claudio's speeches make an interesting pattern. Her speeches end on half-lines, as at lines 63, 65, 70, 73, 76, 84 and 97, and their metrical incompleteness registers both what is left unsaid in her account and a space for him to speak, almost as if she is leaving him a metrical gap in which to reassure her. Instead his responses are increasingly panicky questions, hurrying the story along and clutching at straws (see Textual Analysis, Text 3). She discloses the situation in incremental pieces, and her speech seesaws, like much of the scene, on the words 'life' and 'death'. 'Yes, brother,' she announces, 'you may live' (line 67) and again the cropped line leaves a gap for Claudio's reaction, before she resumes her analysis that such a life would 'fetter you till death' (line 70). As in her discussion with Angelo in II.4, Isabella's perspective on justice is a religious one, and here again her interlocutor has more earthly preoccupations. The comfort she brings is not mortal but heavenly. Claudio interprets her imagery of 'fetters', by which she suggests the fettering of the immortal soul in sin, literally, as 'Perpetual durance' – life imprisonment – and in response Isabella takes back this literal interpretation as a religious **metaphor**. She seems, as he observes fretfully, unable to come to the point plainly, and she admits that she fears to do so. When she does tell him, she is encouraged by his vehemence, but having been given an option of freedom at whatever price he begins to haver. Like Angelo at II.4.63–4, Claudio attempts to realign moral edicts, arguing for a relative rather than an absolute concept of sin: 'Sure it is no sin, / Or of the deadly seven it is the least' (lines 113–4). In his speech on death as 'too horrible' (line 131), Claudio's imagery is all of matter and the elements, of the 'warm motion' turned to 'cold obstruction', of the body imprisoned in fire or ice or winds: like the Duke he has no confidence in an afterlife, still less in a heaven or in God's mercy, but his response is to find 'most loathèd worldly life' (line 132) 'a paradise' (line 134) by comparison. It is a powerful speech with echoes of Hamlet's attempts to make a meaning of his life, and establishes Claudio as a character of real depth and interest (see Characterisation).

Isabella shows no compassion for his fears when set against the price which is demanded for his life, nor does she revert to the Christian concept of comfort with which she began the interview.

Her exclamatory denunciations mark her fury and her brother's attempts to continue the conversation are disregarded. Isabella's discomfiture at her brother's response carries into her initial words with the Duke, where she snappishly tells him she has 'no superfluous leisure'. Both speak in prose, perhaps to register a relaxation of the tension notched up by the tautly interlaced pentameters of the preceding encounter. The Duke's remarks to Claudio are terse and to the point, and, as an audience, we may wonder momentarily whether we ought to believe him. This confusion emphasises the ambiguity of the Duke's character (see Characterisation). His intervention to confirm to Isabella that Claudio's death is imminent seems an unnecessary cruelty at a point when we do not know his overall strategy.

The conversation between the Duke and Isabella conveys a good deal of important plot information, including the introduction of Mariana as a device to solve the tangled situation. The Duke speaks the most, moving matters quickly along, hardly allowing any space for Isabella to question this dubious plan. His orders are clear and detailed, full of imperative verbs of command, almost breathless in their speed and length. The plan demonstrates a level of physical and mental energy that the Duke has not hitherto revealed. At this point he turns from a man who has been characterised by impotence and inactivity, who has let things slip, abdicated his position and taken up the passive role of observer in his own state, into an authoritative figure in active control of an audacious and exciting plot (see Characterisation). He takes Isabella, who seems dazed by her encounter with Claudio and who speaks only a few lines, all characterised by indignant and exclamatory rhetoric, along with him. The scene plays daringly with improbability – why would Isabella agree to place Mariana in a position she so vehemently rejects for herself? Paola Dionisotti, who played Isabella in a production in 1978, argues that the scene works because 'she is so devastated by what has just happened – that horrendous scene with her brother in which everything is severed and smashed – that she is like putty in the Duke's hands. He is madly constructing some framework, throwing some desperate lifeline which, *because* of her desperation, she grabs' (see Critical History & Broader Perspectives; Characterisation). There is some dramatic irony in her vow to tell the Duke, when he returns, how mistaken he has been about Angelo's character. **Peripeteia**, the turn of the plot for the good, is in sight.

In the Folio text there is no scene break at this point, leaving the whole of Act III without a scene change. Scene changes in the Renaissance theatre were prompted by a momentarily empty stage when all the actors from one episode leave to be replaced by a different set of characters. As the Duke remains on stage between Isabella's exit at line 269 and the entrance of Elbow, Pompey and Officers in the next line, there is a clear logic to the Folio arrangement. Played or read without a scene break the sense of the action speeding up would be enhanced.

5 **absolute** resolute

9 **Servile** slave

10 **keep'st** dwell

12–13 **For him ... him still** you try to run away from death but you are always running towards it

14 **accommodations** conveniences

16 **fork** forked tongue

17 **worm** snake

18 **provok'st** invites

23 **certain** constant

29 **bowels** offspring, children
   do call thee sire acknowledge you as father

31 **serpigo** skin disease
   rheum catarrh, discharge

36 **palsied eld** old people afflicted by palsy

37 **heat** energy
   limb strength

40 **more thousand** thousands

62 **lieger** resident ambassador

63 **appointment** preparations

64 **set on** begin a journey

70 **Perpetual durance** life imprisonment

72 **vastidity** vastness

73 **determined scope** defined limit

75 **bark** strip bark from

85 **resolution** determination

92 **appliances** remedies

94 **enew** drive into the water (the image is from falconry)

96 **cast** scoured, purged

99 **invest** clothe

100 **guards** decorative facings or trimmings on the front of a garment

111 **affections** passions

118 **perdurably fined** eternally punished

123 **sensible** sensitive

124 **delighted** capable of feeling delight

126 **thrilling** piercing

127 **viewless** invisible

129 **pendent** hanging, floating

140 **dishonest** lewd, dishonourable

144 **shield** forbid

145 **warpèd slip** contorted shoot, immoral son

    wilderness wildness

146 **defiance** contempt, enmity

157 **dispense** give up

164 **assay** trial

165–6 **practise ... natures** test his ability as a judge of character

185 **complexion** nature

191 **resolve** answer

195 **discover** reveal

    government moral conduct and political rule

198 **avoid** refute

212 **miscarried** died through an accident

223 **sinew** strength

224 **combinate** betrothed

228 **swallowed** retracted

231 **marble** hard, unyielding

235 **avail** benefit

246 **refer yourself to this advantage** place this condition

251 **stead up** fulfil

255 **scaled** weighed as in scales

256 **frame** direct, prepare

261 **perfection** fulfilment

SCENE *2* The disguised Duke denounces Pompey who has been rearrested. Lucio refuses to stand bail for him, and then, in conversation with the 'friar', he slanders the absent Duke as a drunken libertine. Mistress Overdone, also in custody, accuses Lucio of having a child with a woman outside marriage. Escalus praises the Duke to the 'friar', and expresses concern for Claudio

Elbow's reappearance with the still unrepentant and jesting Pompey gives the Duke the chance to address one of his reprobate subjects from the position of his disguise. His denunciation is fierce, and he seems almost to forget himself as friar in the ducal order 'Take him to prison, officer' (line 29). Lucio banters with Pompey, using his name repeatedly in ironic mockery of its noble associations, and bids him off to prison as a bawd. He refuses to be Pompey's bail. When the prison party has exited, Lucio engages the 'friar' in conversation about the absent Duke and about Angelo's behaviour as his deputy. They both agree that Angelo is too severe, and Lucio jokes that he is not even human, so cold is he to physical pleasures. Lucio criticises Angelo's harsh punishment of Claudio, and asserts that the Duke would not have been so sharp, for 'He had some feeling for the sport' (line 113). The Duke tries to defend himself but Lucio claims an intimacy with the Duke which gives him insight into his foibles, adding 'He would be drunk too' (line 121) and that he was not in fact wise as he was held to be, but rather 'very superficial, ignorant, unweighing' (line 132). The Duke finds out Lucio's name. The conversation then turns to Claudio's fate, but this Lucio also brings round to the supposed cupidity of the Duke. When he has left, the Duke speaks angrily of 'back-wounding calumny' (line 176). Mistress Overdone enters in the guard of the officers and Escalus. She begs Escalus for mercy but he is adamant in his sentencing. She says that it is Lucio who has informed on her, and makes a counteraccusation that he has fathered a child with Kate Keepdown. Escalus calls for Lucio to be summoned and despatches her to prison. Escalus exchanges some words

with the disguised Duke, who states that the world is in a critical
condition because goodness is in such short supply. The Duke asks
Escalus 'of what disposition was the Duke?' (lines 220–1), and receives
a more comfortable answer about the Duke's temperance and sobriety.
They discuss Claudio's demeanour in the face of death. The Duke's
final soliloquy reflects on Angelo's hypocritical behaviour and on the
need to employ 'Craft against vice' (line 265) to bring about a just
conclusion.

> This scene seems designed to amplify and corroborate for the Duke
> the news of Angelo's corruption, and to demonstrate the general
> failings of humanity. In parading the reprobate citizens Pompey
> and Mistress Overdone and giving voice to Lucio's defamatory
> opinions of the Duke, this episode prompts the disguised ruler to
> reflect on the sinful state of humanity. The scene is punctuated with
> his remarks on the prevailing moral climate, from his injunction to
> Pompey 'Go mend, go mend' (line 25), to his inclusive couplet on
> the gap between seeming and genuine virtue: 'That we were all, as
> some would seem to be, / Free from our faults, as faults from
> seeming free' (lines 36–7). In his guise as the friar he tells Escalus
> that 'there is so great a fever on goodness' (line 212) everywhere,
> and his response to Lucio's cheery descriptions of a rakish Duke
> is the bitter recognition that 'calumny / The whitest virtue strikes'
> (lines 176–7). Everywhere he looks, he seems to see sinfulness and
> moral depravity and a profound lack of respect for authority. Even
> the prose in which the scene is largely written, apart from a few
> lines of the Duke's, seems to signal a decline in standards and a
> relaxation of formal rules paralleling the moral degeneracy of the
> characters. The Duke's final speech is written in short-lined
> rhyming couplets which stand out from the rest of the play – such
> that many earlier critics considered them, without any external
> justification, to be a non-Shakespearean interpolation. In their
> **gnomic**, sometimes obscure pronouncements, they develop the
> Duke's character (see Characterisation) and present him as a
> **choric** observer of past events and their ethical charge as well
> as an active shaper of the future. They move from supplying
> general maxims about good government to reflections on Angelo's

degraded character and an unusually explicit declaration in the final four lines about what the rest of the play will enact.

Much of the scene's tension and humour derives from the dramatic irony of the other characters' ignorance that this 'friar' is in fact the absented Duke. Lucio unknowingly digs himself deeper and deeper into a hole as he lists the Duke's flaws. How to assess this new perspective on the Duke is difficult. It does not coincide with anything previously stated about his character, although it does provide an explanation – and no alternative explanation is offered – for why the Duke was able to preside over such a protracted descent into vice and lawlessness. Even Escalus's counterview does not quite erase the strength of Lucio's confident slanders, although his considered view that the Duke's prime concern was 'to know himself' offers another insight into his character (see Characterisation). The Duke's incognito encounter with his people does not reflect the image of himself which he desires. Spurred on by what he has learnt through his disguise, he ends the third act of the play with a definite plan of action: the relatively passive, distracted man of the first two acts has taken surreptitious control of the play.

3 **bastard** sweet Spanish wine

4 **stuff** nonsense

5 **two usuries** moneylending and prostitution

8 **fox** fox fur was associated with moneylenders

20 **maw** stomach

38 **cord** hangman's rope and the girdle which is part of the friar's habit

43 **Pygmalion's images** in classical mythology, Pygmalion brought his statues to life by falling in love with them. The image suggests fresh young women whose looks are unspoiled

44–5 **extracting it clutched** stealing a purse, or perhaps suggesting masturbation

46 **tune** fashion

51 **morsel** titbit

Procures pimps

54 **tub** (pun) barrel in which beef is salted; the sweating tub used for the treatment of venereal disease

57 **unshunned** unavoidable

67 **husband** housekeeper

keep the house stay indoors

75 **paint** use cosmetics

88 **fantastical** irrational

97 **extirp** root out, extinguish

102 **sea-maid** mermaid

103 **stockfishes** dried cod

105 **motion generative** sexless puppet

109 **codpiece** baggy flap worn over hose or breeches at the groin, hence the male genitals

115 **detected** known

120 **ducat** gold coin

clack-dish begging bowl, perhaps with a sexual innuendo

124 **inward** intimate friend

130 **greater file of the subject** majority of the populace

132 **unweighing** unthinking, lacking in judgement

134 **helmed** directed

136 **bringings-forth** achievements, creations

138 **unskilfully** in ignorance

156 **opposite** opponent

162 **tun-dish** funnel, with a sexual pun

163 **ungenitured** without genitals

169 **untrussing** untying the lower garments, or urinating

171 **eat mutton on Fridays** religious laws forbade the eating of meat on Friday

mutton prostitute

172 **mouth** kiss

173 **brown bread** coarse bread

175 **mortality** human life

176 **'scape** escape

190 **information** legal complaint or charge

193 **Philip and Jacob** the saints' day falls on 1 May

194 **abuse** slander

200 **brother** fellow, colleague

213 **dissolution** destruction

214–16 **it is as ... any undertaking** the meaning seems to be that inconstancy is now a virtue

217 **security** standing as bail or surety

222 **strifes** objectives
228 **events** outcomes
232 **sinister** unjust
240 **shore** limit
258 **my vice** the vice I have allowed to flourish
261–4 **How may … things** cryptic, possibly corrupt lines from which only the most
general sense of the Duke's fulmination against hypocrisy can be deduced
263 **strings** threads
270 **perform** bring to fruition
contracting betrothal

ACT IV

SCENE 1   The Duke introduces Isabella to Mariana. The details of
how Isabella has arranged to meet Angelo are revealed.
Assured by the 'friar' that her compliance is no sin,
Mariana agrees to the plan

The scene begins with music and lyrics which seem to emphasise
unrequited love. The Duke arrives in his friar's disguise, in which he has
clearly often visited Mariana to act as her comforter (see Treatment of
Time), and they exchange some words. The Duke indicates he may need
to speak further with Mariana. Isabella comes with news of her planned
rendezvous with the lustful Angelo that night at the gate of his walled
garden. The plan is moving ahead, but Mariana still knows nothing of it.
The Duke indicates that Isabella will tell her, and the two women
withdraw for the discussion. The Duke briefly reflects again on rank and
worth. Isabella and Mariana return, having agreed the plan. Isabella
reminds her to mention Claudio as she leaves Angelo, and the Duke
reassures her that as 'He is your husband on a pre-contract' (line 71) there
is no sin involved in the deed.

Mariana's agreement to the plan is crucial to the success of the
Duke's machinations, and here she gives no demur. Nor does
Isabella, to whom the job of presenting the proposal is delegated
by the Duke. Both these acceptances are strange, and draw attention
to the play's governing symmetry (see Themes, on Symmetry &

Antithesis). For Mariana is being asked to behave as Juliet has and for which Juliet is being punished. The premarital betrothal which Claudio claimed for himself and Juliet in I.2.144–48 has provided no mitigation for his offence, but here the existence of the same kind of contract between Mariana and Angelo is held to justify their sexual liaison. What was a capital sin in Claudio is 'no sin' (line 72) for Mariana. Isabella's willingness to connive with this plan adds to the complexity of her moral character (see Characterisation), and she expresses no squeamishness at all about retaining her own chastity at the expense of another woman's. She even reminds Mariana to mention 'her brother' (line 69) when she leaves Angelo's bed. Mariana's own characterisation in the scene is sketchy. She speaks only a few lines, and those which have the potential to be the most interesting, her response to the plan, are not heard. It seems a deliberate marginalisation of her as a human being: she is just a function, another body (see Themes, on Substitution), in whom we cannot afford to become too interested or her role will become too difficult to sustain. The Duke ends the scene, as he did Act III, with another promise of active resolution, using the natural imagery of fruition and harvest previously used by Lucio to describe Claudio and Juliet's affair (I.4.40–4), serving again to emphasise the parallels between Angelo and Mariana and Claudio and Juliet.

27 **circummured** walled around

29 **planchèd** planked

30 **his** its

39 **all of precept** by verbal instruction (i.e. not by taking her there)

41 **observance** compliance

42 **repair** visit

43 **possessed** told
   most utmost, longest

46 **stays** waits

61 **contrarious quests** conflicting enquiries

62 **escapes** outbursts

64 **rack** distort, misinterpret

71 **pre-contract** a contract of marriage

74 **flourish** decorate

75 **tilth** arable land

SCENE 2   In the prison, Pompey is appointed to assist the
executioner Abhorson. Angelo's order to execute Claudio
is reiterated: his head is to be sent to Angelo in the
morning. The disguised Duke persuades the Provost to
spare Claudio and instead send the head of Barnadine, a
convicted murderer

The Provost arranges for Pompey to assist the executioner Abhorson at
the executions of Claudio and Barnadine in return for a reduction of his
sentence. Abhorson exchanges a few laconic words with his new assistant
who is still full of puns and bawdy jokes. The Provost expresses his pity
for Claudio, but not for Barnadine as a murderer. Claudio tells him that
Barnadine is sleeping, and the Provost wishes Claudio comfort as he
prepares for his death. The Duke in his friar's disguise comes to visit the
Provost, and defends Angelo's actions as the 'great justice' of one who is
innocent of the crimes he punishes in others, allowing that 'Were he
mealed with that / Which he corrects, then were he tyrannous' (lines
81–2). The Duke tells the Provost that a pardon for Claudio is likely to
arrive, and, on cue, a messenger appears. The Duke appears to anticipate
that Angelo will keep his side of the bargain, having slept, as he believes,
with Isabella. The message, however, is that Claudio is to be executed by
four o'clock and that his head is to be sent to Angelo within an hour. The
Duke asks the Provost about Barnadine's situation and character, and
hears that this prisoner is impenitent of his crime and has no fear of
death. The Duke tells the Provost to spare Claudio's life and execute
Barnadine, and to send his head, shaved to look more like that of
Claudio, to Angelo. The Provost demurs at this action which 'is against
my oath' (line 176), but the Duke persuades him that the Duke, to whom
the Provost swore his oath, would approve his actions and shows him a
letter with the ducal seal and signature to add weight to this promise. He
continues to persuade and reassure him.

In this prison scene we see the Duke's plans coming closer to
fruition, as he introduces the expedient device of sending another
man's head in place of Claudio's (see Themes, on Substitution).

The first half of the scene is concerned with the dark humour of the
interchange between the pointedly named Abhorson (his name
puns on 'abhor' as well as on 'whore's son') and the irrepressible
Pompey. Pompey makes much merriment on a joke linking
beheading with the taking of women's maidenheads, or virginity,
thereby allying his current and former occupations. The true cost of
this 'mystery' or executioner's craft is demonstrated with Claudio's
short appearance. He says nothing about himself or his own feelings
as he waits for morning and death: after his anguished eloquence in
III.1 he seems spent, and he does not speak again in the play after
this short interchange with the Provost. The Duke's entrance is
cheery – inappropriately so – and he seems to be enjoying his new
active role in setting the tangled situation to rights. His speech
about Angelo's justness as a man who punishes crimes and appetites
which he himself restrains is heavily ironic: the Duke and the
audience know that this is far from the truth. His apparent defence
of the deputy, therefore, is an implicit accusation. His response to
Angelo's message about Claudio's execution shows him thinking
quickly and creatively. Having expected a pardon, he quickly
regains control of events as he establishes the suitability of
Barnadine as a substitute for Claudio. His long prose speeches show
him talking over any opposition to his plans, as he did when
proposing the bed-trick plan to Isabella in III.1. The Duke
overrides the Provost's misgivings with the authority of the
(supposedly absent) Duke. For the first time in the play, therefore,
we see the Duke use his authority, albeit by a kind of proxy, and this
may mark a promise of more active and just government in the
future. References to the dawn at the end of the scene draw
attention to the quickening time-scale of events (see Treatment of
Time).

4 **wife's head** (pun) the man as head of the household, and 'maidenhead' =
virginity

6 **snatches** jokes

11 **gyves** shackles, fetters

21 **compound** make terms

24 **estimation** reputation

26 **mystery** profession

40 **true** honest

40–4 **Every true ... your thief** a garbled exposition based on the hangman's traditional right to the clothes of his victims, and punning on 'fits' = is the right size for and is appropriate to

55 **yare** prepared

good turn 'turning off' was the act of execution

64 **starkly** stiffly

75 **bitter** severe

77 **Even with** in conformity with

80 **mealed** stained

84 **steelèd** hardened

86 **unsisting** unassisting

postern back gate or door

89 **countermand** reprieve

95 **siege** seat

114 **putting on** urging, incitement

128 **nine years old** for nine years

133 **fact** crime

134 **undoubtful** certain

142 **desperately mortal** in a desperate state of mortal sin

153 **in hazard** in a dangerous position

156 **manifested** revealed

161 **limited** prescribed

168 **discover the favour** recognise the face

173 **fall** happen

184 **attempt** persuade

187 **character** handwriting

196 **unfolding star** morning star

202 **resolve** reassure

SCENE 3   Barnadine, drunk and unrepentant, refuses to attend his execution. Instead, the head of Ragozine who has died of fever is to be sent to Angelo in place of that of Claudio. The Duke plans to summon Angelo to meet him on his 'return' the next day. He tells Isabella that Claudio has been executed, and arranges for her to meet the Duke next day to denounce Angelo publicly

Pompey gives a disreputable commentary on the prison inmates and he and Abhorson call Barnadine for his execution. With much cursing Barnadine indicates his unpreparedness: 'I have been drinking all night. I am not fitted for't' (lines 41–2). The Duke attempts to persuade him but Barnadine is adamant, and it is decided that it would be 'damnable' – both for Barnadine and for his captors – to execute him while he is in this unrepentant mood. Fortunately, the Provost can reveal that there has been a death from illness in the prison, that of Ragozine, 'a most notorious pirate' (line 69) and a man who even resembles Claudio in colouring. He suggests that Ragozine's head should be sent as Claudio's, and the Duke agrees that this opportunity is heaven-sent. He persuades the Provost to keep both Barnadine and Claudio from execution, promising that within two days the rightness of the course of action will be proved. The Duke plans to send letters announcing his return and bidding one Varrius to meet him to arrange his return. The Provost is despatched to Angelo with the head.

    Isabella arrives at the prison to ask for her brother. In a brief soliloquy prompted by her approach, the Duke reveals that he 'will keep her ignorant of her good'. Instead he tells Isabella that Claudio has been executed and his head sent to Angelo. She cannot believe this at first, but the Duke proposes a focus for her anger – the return of the Duke the next day. He bids her go and meet him at the city gate and she will gain 'revenges' (line 134). He also sends her with a letter to Friar Peter bidding him come to Mariana's house. He leaves Isabella in the care of Friar Peter, telling her that he himself will not be present at the Duke's return as he is 'combinèd by a sacred vow' (line 142). Lucio enters, and commiserates with Isabella, stating that if the 'old fantastical Duke of dark corners had been at home' (lines 155–6), Claudio would not have been executed. Lucio tells the disguised

Duke more about the character of the Duke, and admits that, being brought before him on a charge of getting a woman pregnant, he denied it.

The Duke's plans continue apace. When Isabella complies 'I am directed by you' (line 135), her statement has a more extensive reference than her immediate orders from the friar. The Duke's active control of the plot has subsumed all action by other characters, who seem reduced to trusting to this mysterious 'friar' and carrying out his commands. Isabella, in particular, is a shadow of her former vociferous and assertive self (see Characterisation). One character, however, bucks this submissive trend. Barnadine's uncompromising refusal to be executed blocks the Duke's plans and poses a challenge to his plotting. Barnadine declines to be a piece in the Duke's jigsaw, and his unrepentant and unbowed presence in the scene offers a radical alternative to the pious observations of the Duke and Provost. He gains a stay of execution through this determination, but the Duke's plans are hardly interrupted because of the happy coincidence of Ragozine's death. Ragozine enters the play as the substitute for a substitute (see Themes, on Substitution), but the ease of this second replacement casts Barnadine's role into interesting relief. A more streamlined plot would have excised Barnadine's part altogether: if all that is needed is a dead head to stand in for that of Claudio's, the final solution, that of Ragozine's death from fever, would be ideal, without any need for the added complication of Barnadine. That this simpler course was not chosen by Shakespeare means that Barnadine's role is important not primarily as a plot device but as a challenge to the play's prevailing codes of repentance of crime and submission to authority. His behaviour amplifies Pompey's jaunty volubility earlier in the scene and makes his ultimate fate in Act V all the more significant. There are some characters who, it seems, will never submit to the moral or social authority of those in power (see Themes, on Crime, Punishment & Justice).

2 **house of profession** brothel

4 **commodity** usurers, whose profits were limited by law, increased them by paying some of the loan as commodities which the borrower was supposed

to sell to realise the cash. Frequently, as in Master Rash's case, the commodities were of low value and difficult to sell

4 **brown paper** coarse paper

5 **marks** a mark was worth 13*s*. 4*d*.

11 **peaches** impeaches

15 **tilter** jouster

17 **doers in our trade** clients of the brothel

39 **clap into** hurry with

46 **ghostly father** confessor

53 **billets** sticks

61 **ward** cell

71 **omit** leave aside

76 **presently** immediately

77 **Prefixed** stipulated

82 **continue** preserve

87 **journal** daily

yond generation perhaps referring to those beyond the dark prison

89 **free** willing

98 **cold gradation** gradually and deliberately

117 **close** silent

127 **covent** convent

128 **instance** indication

131 **pace** control

133 **your bosom** your wishes

140 **perfect** tell the full story

141 **to the head** in front

143 **combinèd** bound

151 **fain** forced

152 **for my head** for fear of being beheaded

155 **fantastical** eccentric, whimsical

156 **dark corners** furtive, secretive

157 **beholding** indebted

160 **woodman** hunter, chaser after women

170 **medlar** prostitute

SCENE 4 Angelo and Escalus discuss the Duke's letters, which instruct them to meet him at the city gates to hand over his authority. Angelo soliloquises on actions he believes he has committed in having sex with Isabella and having Claudio executed

Angelo and Escalus discuss the Duke's 'uneven and distracted' (line 2) letters and Angelo expresses the hope that 'his wisdom be not tainted' (lines 3–4). They are commanded to proclaim the Duke's return and that if 'any crave redress of injustice' (line 8) they are to do so publicly at that time. Escalus observes that this is to protect his deputies against complaints later. Alone, Angelo fears that the 'deflowered maid' (line 19) may use this opportunity to denounce him, but comforts himself with the thought of his own authority which is immune to scandal. Angelo goes on to express regret at Claudio's death: 'Would yet he had lived' (line 30).

Angelo has not been on stage since the end of Act II: this scene shows something of his response to his subsequent actions. The news of the Duke's arrangements for his return throws Angelo into guilty anxiety. Will Isabella take advantage of the Duke's proclamation to condemn him? But while Angelo's primary concern is for his own escape from censure, this soliloquy is revelatory of his divided feelings. He cannot quite bring himself to admit to what he believes he has done, preferring the third-person circumlocution of 'by an eminent body that enforced / The law against it' (lines 20–1), but this evasive formulation does recognise the hypocrisy of his behaviour. Again, it seems that Angelo cannot bring himself to speak the name of Claudio, or perhaps his thoughts do not need such labels, but he does seem to admit that his death was wrong. The final couplet sums up Angelo's disjointed response: 'we would, and we would not' (line 32) (see Characterisation).

1 **disvouched** contradicted
5 **reliver** hand over
10 **dispatch** prompt settlement
11 **devices** plots
15 **of sort and suit** those of rank and in attendance

18 **unshapes me** destroys my self-possession
unpregnant unready
19 **dull** unresponsive
20 **eminent body** public figure
23 **dares her no** she would not dare
24 **credent bulk** weighty and respectable
25 **particular** personal
27 **sense** sensuality

SCENE 5   **The Duke instructs Friar Peter who is helping arrange the public denunciation**

The Duke appears in his own clothing and makes plans for his return. He sends Friar Peter to gather together various individuals for this grand repossession of his ducal authority.

> The Duke continues to give orders as the sequence of short scenes speeds up the pace of the play towards its **dénouement**. He stresses to Friar Peter that he must keep faith with his plan, although we are not given any detail of how the Duke intends to conduct his public interview with Angelo or how matters will be resolved.

1 **deliver me** deliver for me
3 **keep** follow
4 **drift** plan
5 **blench** deviate
6 **minister** suggest

SCENE 6   **Isabella discusses the 'friar's' plan with Mariana. Isabella has misgivings about accusing Angelo of having had sex with her**

Isabella wants Mariana to accuse Angelo, but has been instructed by the disguised Duke to do it herself. She has been reassured that all will come right, even if the 'friar' seems to oppose her. Friar Peter arrives with news that they have an excellent position in the crowd from which to address the Duke. The trumpets have announced that he will very soon enter the gates of the city.

In the previous scene the Duke urged Friar Peter to stick to the plan even if events seem to be going against them. Here Isabella indicates that she has been given similar advice by the 'friar'. Both scenes serve to raise the tension about how the play will be resolved, and with these hints about how the final showdown will be managed, the stage is set for the culmination of the Duke's plotting. Mariana's advice 'Be ruled by him' (line 4) emphasises the Duke's control of events: whereas earlier Isabella had been his accomplice in persuading Mariana to his plan now she is ignorant – reduced to one of the pawns the Duke is moving on the great chessboard of his strategy.

4 **to veil full purpose** to conceal the plan

7 **physic** medicine

10 **stand** position

13 **generous** highest ranking

14 **hent** reached

    near upon shortly

Act V

SCENE 1   **Back in his rightful clothes, and before a crowd of people, the Duke meets Angelo and Escalus at the city gate. Through testimony by Isabella and Mariana, and the return of the Duke in the friar's disguise, the truth about Angelo is revealed. He is commanded to marry Mariana, and the Duke agrees to spare his life when Isabella and Mariana plead for mercy. Claudio is brought in and reminded to marry Juliet. Lucio is sentenced to death but this is commuted to marrying Kate Keepdown. The Duke proposes marriage to Isabella**

The Duke returns and is greeted by Angelo and Escalus and a crowd of other citizens. He congratulates them on their conduct of government during his absence, and announces that he has heard much good of their 'justice'. He makes a speech of public thanks to Angelo. Isabella, prompted by Friar Peter, addresses the Duke and begs him to hear her story and give her justice. The Duke replies that she should seek this from Angelo, but she begs him. Angelo tries to pre-empt her by indicating to the Duke that she may be mad. Isabella denounces Angelo as 'An hypocrite, a virgin-violator' (line 41). The Duke seems to dismiss her, but her story gains his interest and she gives the details of Claudio's fate. Lucio attempts to intervene but is repeatedly silenced by the Duke. The Duke makes to send Isabella to prison, and calls for the 'meddling friar' who has prompted her to make these accusations. Lucio tells the Duke that the friar has spoken against him during his absence. Friar Peter tells the Duke that the friar cannot be summoned because he is ill, and defends him against Lucio's imputations. The Duke appears not to be taking this seriously, asking Angelo, 'Do you not smile at this' (line 163).

Mariana enters, veiled, and is interrogated by the Duke. She admits that she is unmarried but is not a maid: 'I have known my husband, yet my husband / Knows not that ever he knew me' (lines 196–7). Lucio continues to interrupt and is severely reprimanded by the Duke. Mariana names Angelo as her husband and unveils herself, telling the story of the 'bed-trick'. The Duke asks Angelo if this is true. Angelo admits that there was 'some speech of marriage' (line 215) between them but that it was broken off due to Mariana's stained reputation, and he asserts that he has had no contact with her for five years. Angelo tells the Duke that he is the victim of some orchestrated smear by 'some more mightier member' (line 235) than his female accusers, and the Duke gives him authority to punish them, ordering that the friar be sent for. The Duke leaves Angelo to deal with the slanders and makes his exit.

After a few comments from Lucio and Escalus's summoning of Isabella to speak again, the Duke returns in his friar's disguise. Escalus interrogates him and accuses him of slandering Angelo. The disguised Duke describes what he has seen as 'a looker-on here in Vienna' (line 315). Lucio faces the friar and repeats his allegations that he has heard him call the duke 'a fleshmonger, a fool, and a coward' (line 332). There is an altercation as Lucio pulls off the friar's hood to reveal the Duke, who promptly orders Lucio's arrest. The Duke questions Angelo who admits his faults and begs to be put to death. He is ordered to marry Mariana. Turning to Isabella, the Duke admits that she may wonder why he did not reveal himself sooner and save her brother. Angelo and Mariana are returned, 'new-married' (line 397) and the Duke announces that as requital for the death of Claudio, Angelo must die. Mariana pleads for clemency, and begs Isabella to join in her pleas. She consents and kneels before the Duke, arguing that Angelo's crime was only intended, whereas Claudio deserved his punishment for the enacting of his desires. The Duke hears from the Provost that the order to execute Claudio came privately, and for this disregard of the regulatory procedures, he deprives the Provost of his office. He is sent to bring Barnadine. Escalus expresses his disappointment that Angelo 'should slip so grossly' (line 469), to which Angelo replies that he craves 'death more willingly than mercy (line 473). Barnadine and Claudio, his face covered, are brought, as is Juliet.

The Duke pardons Barnadine and bids him live a better life. He then orders that Claudio be uncovered and returns him to Isabella. The Duke asks her to marry him. He announces Angelo's pardon and tells him to 'love your wife' (line 494), and then turns to Lucio. He orders that if there is any woman who has had a child by Lucio, she is to come forward and he will marry her, and then be hanged. Lucio objects, and the Duke moderates the sentence to marriage alone, which Lucio describes as worse than death. 'Slandering a prince deserves it' (line 521) is the Duke's imperious reply. A series of orders – to Claudio to marry Juliet, to Mariana to be happy and to Angelo to love his wife, thanks to Escalus and to the Provost who is promised a better job – ends with the Duke's second proposal to Isabella. She makes no verbal response.

> This long scene is the culmination of the Duke's plans. All the major characters appear, and are arranged on the stage and dealt their varying punishments. The strain of juggling all the strands of the plot may show at certain points – the Duke cannot think of a good reason why he has to withdraw in order to return as the friar, for example – but he withholds and reveals information with the theatrical delight of a conjuror. Having set up this **dénouement** where all the main characters will meet, the Duke presides with evident enjoyment. All his 'actors' play their parts as they have been told, and the play ends with the marriages characteristic of the finale of Shakespearean comedy. There are, however, some distinct and deafening silences. Neither Claudio nor Juliet speaks in the scene, despite being addressed by the Duke. Angelo makes scant

response to his enforced marriage and to his escape from death. Barnadine gives no reaction to the unexpected news of his pardon. And most tellingly of all, Isabella treats the Duke's two offers of marriage with absolute silence. These silences act as wordless questions, gaps in the script of the play which can only be filled by our interpretation of the scene and the whole play. How do these characters react to their different situations at the end of the play? Shakespeare's conclusion leaves certain issues unresolved, and it is for the director of the play in performance to decide, for example, whether Isabella accepts the Duke's proposal, or whether it looks likely that Angelo will love Mariana as he is commanded. Optimists might choose to read silences as a sign of inaudible gratitude; cynics may find them fertile breeding grounds of dissent at the Duke's interventions. Is his behaviour justified? Why does he manipulate the disclosure of information to the last moment? Does he behave justly in his final apportioning of advice, punishment, and lenity?

'Justice' is a word which echoes through the scene. Isabella, the Duke, Angelo and Mariana all use it as the play focuses on one of its key themes in this public arraignment. Through repetition, however, the word itself and the abstract concept it denotes become strained, until it is hard to come to any conclusion about what justice is. Would it be just for Angelo to be killed in punishment for the death of Claudio? Is it just to suggest that he should be, while knowing that Claudio is not in fact dead? Is it just to redeem the irredeemable Barnadine? Is it just to dispense marriage as a punishment, as the Duke does to both Angelo and Lucio? Should 'slandering a prince' earn whipping? The Duke uses a formulation which seems to express equivalence and balance, and refers to the play's title: 'An Angelo for Claudio, death for death' (line 406), 'Like doth quit like, and Measure still for Measure' (line 408) (see Themes, on Symmetry & Antithesis). The image of justice as a balanced set of scales is implicit in this rhetorical arrangement. But the play encourages us to question this apparent neatness, and the justness of such cold legalistic substitutions (see Themes, on Substitution). It could be argued that the Duke's dispensing of justice represents the ideal of severity tempered with mercy, a Christian ideal, or his desire to see the women beg for Angelo may appear to be a dubious assertion of his legal power (see Characterisation).

Isabella's pleas for Angelo demonstrate the extent of her development through the play. As a novice in the convent she was to dedicate her life to God; here she kneels to an earthly ruler for mercy for a condemned man. Her speech rhythms may indicate her unwillingness: a series of monosyllables, a short line at 447, a philosophically and theologically dubious distinction between sinful thoughts and actions. (Isabella contradicts New Testament teaching on the equivalence of intent and action: 'You have heard that it was said by them of old time, Thou shalt not commit adultery: But I say unto you, That whosoever looketh on a woman to lust after her hath committed adultery with her already in his heart' (Matthew 5:27–8).) Elsewhere in the play we have heard her passionate eloquence (II.2, II.4, III.1); by comparison this is forced and unconvincing (see Characterisation). Angelo himself is monotone: when the truth is revealed, he wishes only for death. His muted and self-accusing demeanour seems an unsatisfactory basis for marriage, and Mariana's continued faith in him may stretch our credulity. We can only interpret this marriage as a 'happy ending' with a determined suppression of our doubts and misgivings. Lucio's involvement in the scene is as a cheeky commentator, interrupting the solemn proceedings with a stream of one-liners which threaten to steal the limelight from the principals. His treatment may seem particularly harsh, and it is striking that the Duke reserves his harshest words and punishment not for the hypocritical ruler or the convicted murderer but for the man whom he heard slander him. Lucio's transgression in getting Kate Keepdown pregnant serves as a miniature recapitulation of the themes of the play: sex before marriage recalls both Claudio and Angelo, execution for fornication faced also Claudio, and marrying as a punishment with the threat of execution parallels Angelo (see Themes, on Symmetry & Antithesis).

The play's final words are the Duke's promise of revelation: 'So, bring us to our palace, where we'll show / What's yet behind, that's meet you all should know' (lines 535–6). What can he be planning to disclose which has not come to light in this lengthy scene? It is characteristic of the play's tantalising mode that it closes with a hint that we do not, and now never will, know the full story. Effectively, then, the ending is deferred, and it will happen out of our view. Like the Duke himself, the play is effective through managing knowledge and information, and this concluding couplet firmly reminds us that there is always more to know.

1 **cousin** courtesy form of address to a fellow nobleman

8 **Forerunning more requital** preceding other rewards

   bonds obligations

10 **wards of covert bosom** the innermost heart

11 **characters** letters

12 **forted** fortified

13 **razure** erasure

16 **keep** dwell

20 **Vail your regard** lower your eyes

30–1 **for that ... believed** if it is not believed I will be punished (for slander)

48 **conjure** plead

50–1 **That thou ... madness** do not ignore me because you think I am mad

52 **unlike** improbable

54 **absolute** perfect

55 **dressings** robes

   characts symbols or badges of rank

   titles official positions

   forms ceremonies

65 **inequality** injustice

66 **seems** that seems

72 **probation** period of testing before entry to religious order

81 **A business for yourself** your own business

82 **perfect** well-prepared

91 **Mended** corrected

92 **needless** unnecessary, useless

94 **refelled** refused

98 **concup'sible** burning with desire

   intemperate ungoverned

100 **remorse** compassion

100 **confutes** overcomes

104 **like** probable

105 **fond** foolish

106 **suborned** prompted by another party to make false accusations

107 **practice** conspiracy

108 **it imports no reason** it does not make sense

115 **ministers** angels

117 **Unfold** reveal

118 **countenance** outward show, acceptance

122 **blasting** defaming

128 **lay** not a friar

130 **swinged** beaten

131 **This'** this is

135 **saucy** insolent

136 **scurvy** worthless

141 **touch or soil** moral stain

142 **ungot** not yet conceived

145 **temporary meddler** one interfering in worldly (temporal) affairs

148 **misreport** slander

152 **mere** sole

157 **probation** proof

     make up full clear establish clearly as the truth

158 **convented** summoned

160 **vulgarly** publicly

164 **vanity** futility

179 **punk** prostitute

181 **cause** charge, accusation

186 **known** had sexual relations with

197 **all th'effect of love** full sexual intercourse

203 **abuse** deceit

209 **match** appointment

210 **supply thee** satisfy your desires

217 **proportions** dowry

218 **composition** the agreed sum

219 **disvalued** destroyed

220 **levity** wanton behaviour

230 **confixèd** fastened

232 **scope** full extent

SCENE 1 continued

233 **touched** wounded

234 **informal** demented

235 **member** person

240 **Compact** conspirator

241 **particular** individual

243 **sealed in approbation** sealed with official endorsement

254 **injuries** wrongs against you

256–7 **well / Determinèd** made a careful judgement

261 ***Cucullus non facit monachum*** (proverbial) the hood does not make the monk

265 **enforce** use, urge

266 **notable** notorious

277 **darkly** cryptically

278 **light** randy

290–1 **Respect to ... burning throne** I respect your authority, as is even due to the devil for his splendid throne

297 **Good night to your redress** bid farewell to justice

299 **retort** reject

303 **unreverend** irreverent
unhallowed unholy

307 **glance** allude

308 **tax him** accuse him

309 **touse** tear

311 **hot** hasty

314 **provincial** subject to local laws

319 **forfeits in a barber's shop** it seems that barbers had lists of mock-penalties for misbehaviour by customers, but since barbers also acted as surgeons and dentists, their forfeits, or items set up as an example to others, might be more grisly

330 **notedly** particularly

331 **fleshmonger** fornicator

339 **close** compromise

344 **giglots** lewd women

351 **sheep-biting** of the proverbial wolf in sheep's clothing, sneaking, deceitful
hanged dogs that worried sheep were hanged

353 **mad'st** created

361 **do thee office** be of service to you

365 **undiscernible** imperceptible

367 **passes** events, trespasses

370 **sequent** consequent

375 **consummate** completed

380 **Advertising** attentive

   holy dedicated

382 **Attorneyed** bound

383 **vassal** servant

389 **rash remonstrance** hasty revelation

393 **brained** killed

398 **salt** lecherous

404 **very mercy** most merciful aspects

405 **proper** very

414 **mock** tantalise

417 **imputation** accusation, rumour

424 **definitive** immovable

430 **sense** reason

432 **pavèd bed** grave

450 **subjects** deeds

460 **knew it not** was not certain

461 **advice** reflection

468 **still** hitherto

469 **blood** sexual appetite

479 **squar'st** conducts

480 **quit** remit, pardon

492 **quickening** revival

493 **quits** requites

495 **apt remission** willing forgiveness

498 **luxury** lechery

502 **trick** joke or whim

517 **Remit thy other forfeits** cancel your other punishments

519 **pressing to death** form of torture in which the prisoner was pressed with heavy weights until he pleaded or died

524 **confessed** heard her confession

526 **more behind** more to follow

   gratulate pleasing

532 **motion** proposal

   imports your good will bring you great benefit

PART THREE

CRITICAL APPROACHES

CHARACTERISATION

Characters in a play are just that: characters. It may seem obvious to say that they are not real people and that they should not be discussed as such. They consist of what they say and what is said about them: they are composed of words, not of flesh and blood, nor of inner psychology. It is significant that the very word 'character' derives from words denoting marking or writing (as in its uses in *Measure for Measure*, for example at V.1.11), only gaining its modern meanings of 'individual personality' or 'person in a play' in the late seventeenth century. Sometimes Shakespearean characters have a representative, rather than an individual function: they embody behaviours or conditions as symbolic personifications. Sometimes naming can be a clue to this: the names 'Angelo', for example, or even 'Abhorson', have clear symbolic connotations (whereas the name 'Isabella' does not). Some characters exist as dramatic devices rather than as fully realised individuals. It is difficult to deduce much about Mariana except, perhaps, that there is nothing to deduce about her beyond her role in the Duke's scheme. Similarly, Barnadine is an irrelevant character in plot terms – it would be much more streamlined to have Ragozine's fortuitous death as the answer to Angelo's demand for the head of Claudio (see Themes, on Substitution) than to introduce an intermediate character. The reasons for Barnadine's presence in the play, therefore, may be seen as more symbolic: he represents an unregenerate and extreme form of immorality and thus his pardon at the end of the play needs to be examined alongside those of the others.

At other points Shakespeare's gift for recognisable and distinctive characterisation is evident: single phrases or gestures can suggest an entire personality. In performance the assumptions of the **Method** school tend to dominate, whereby the inner motivations of the characters – their life beyond what is written for them in the play – are a crucial part of directors' and actors' interpretation. These notes on characters use information from performances where it offers a particular slant, but they also try to remember that Shakespeare's characters derive from an age in which personality and the sense of the individual were quite different from now, and especially that they are part of a theatrical culture in which **verisimilitude** is not always the prime concern. Shakespeare's concern with balance and symmetry in this play (see Themes, on Symmetry & Antithesis) also means that characters should not only be analysed as distinct individuals but also in different combinations and comparisons. Characterisation forms part of the overall structure of the play, and should not be considered in isolation from its themes and language.

THE DUKE

How the Duke's character is interpreted has a crucial effect on the interpretation of the whole play. Is he, as Lucio avers, a 'Duke of dark corners' (IV.3.156) or does he bear 'the sword of heaven' (III.2.249)? Is his 'ethical attitude exactly correspondent with Jesus', as the critic G. Wilson Knight has suggested, or is he a Machiavellian powermonger who moves unseen and all-seeing among his people in order better to dominate them, as has been argued by Richard Wilson (see Critical History & Broader Perspectives)? These interpretations locate the Duke in two different plays. A Christ-like Duke brings about a redemptive happy ending; a political manipulator is out for himself. As this Note has attempted to argue throughout, the interest of the questions and problems thrown up by *Measure for Measure* lies in their possibilities rather than decisive interpretations: what is interesting and significant about the characterisation of the Duke is that it can sustain such diverse readings.

The Duke's first appearance in I.1 is mysterious. Why is he leaving and why does he promote the untested Angelo? His speeches are lengthy and reflective, turning to the philosophical, and sometimes difficult to penetrate. They are not the direct and purposeful instructions of an efficient ruler making preparations for an unavoidable absence. Perhaps the syntax represents mental unease: the breakdown of order in the state may be reflected, or may itself reflect a breakdown in the Duke. (The physical and moral health of the nation and of its ruler were often allied in Renaissance political philosophy.) There are suggestions that he longs for solitude as he declines any ceremony on his departure: 'I love the people, / But do not like to stage me to their eyes' (I.1.67–8). This is a repeated theme of the Duke's character: he tells Friar Thomas in I.3 that he has 'ever loved the life removed' (line 8), and in IV.1, while Isabella discusses his plan with Mariana, the Duke soliloquises, apparently unprompted, on the 'millions of false eyes' which are stuck on 'place and greatness' (line 59). Perhaps the Duke's adoption of a disguise by which he can move about, seeing but unseen, hidden from view by the cowl of his habit, is his attempt to redress the disadvantage of his public role. Instead of being a spectacle to be looked at, his is the seeing eye. Like a mirror he turns back the looks of those who would look at him and makes them look at themselves. This may have sinister implications: many recent critics have discussed the Duke's preoccupation with covert surveillance of his population as a form of tyrannical power (see Critical History & Broader Perspectives), or it may be seen to enforce the associations of the Duke with an omniscient, all-seeing divinity.

As with so much of his behaviour, the Duke's motives for abdicating his office are opaque. Lucio boasts 'I believe I know the cause of his withdrawing' (III.2.125), but then keeps the suspense ''Tis a secret must be locked within the teeth and lips' (line 128). The play seems to acknowledge the gap in explanation for this crucial step: in the first act the Duke promises further elaboration 'at our more leisure' (I.3.49), and at the play's conclusion he is still harping on the story yet to be told: 'So bring us to our palace, where we'll show / What's yet behind, that's meet you all should know' (V.1.536). The Duke tells Friar Thomas that it is not love which prompts his actions. His description of a 'complete bosom' (line 3) suggests an emotional self-sufficiency, which he echoes in his disguise as the friar in the face of Lucio's accusations, claiming that the Duke was 'not inclined' (III.2.116) towards sexual activity. His treatment of Lucio, however, seems to suggest that he is not as 'complete' as he might like to be, and that he is affected by other people's opinions. He seeks reassurance from Escalus after Lucio's tirade. The Duke tells Friar Thomas that he has a 'purpose / More grave and wrinkled than the aims and ends / Of burning youth' (I.3.5–6) (although his view of a happy ending for himself seems to include marriage to Isabella), and he goes on to suggest three reasons, including the desire for seclusion, for his retirement from office, He discusses the way the law has fallen into disuse, and argues that, having presided over its decline, he cannot justly reinforce it, and he also suggests that he wants to test Angelo and see 'if power change purpose, what our seemers be' (I.3.54). This last reason may hint at a more manipulative, Machiavellian, side to his character and a cavalier attitude to the casualties of Angelo's regime. If he already suspects Angelo, it is surely ethically questionable to allow him the power to abuse the Viennese populace. If the whole play is set up as a test for Angelo, however, its other characters are also subjected to testing, even the Duke himself. Roger Allam, who played the Duke for the Royal Shakespeare Company in 1987, felt that he 'constantly uses other people, Angelo, Claudio, Isabella, even Lucio, as a means of self-knowledge': through them he gains understanding of himself.

The idea that the Duke is on a quest for self-knowledge is commonly asserted. For Daniel Massey, another RSC Duke (in 1983), 'a gesture as immense as handing over the reins of power to a young and relatively inexperienced Angelo must go hand in hand, I felt, with some sort of psychological crisis. Perhaps it is an act of desperation. In any event, I divined ... a passionate desire to put things right.' Roger Allam agreed with this line of interpretation, arguing that his character 'seemed to be in the midst of a deep personal crisis about the value of life itself.' The sense of paralysis brought on by this philosophical and psychological dilemma was indicated in this production's presentation of the opening scene, where the Duke sat 'transfixed, staring into space, while around him civil servants were trying to get him to sign important papers'. Both these Dukes, then, leave their office to pursue some personal goal, to set off on a journey of self-discovery through and during which they work out their roles and responsibilities. The play certainly sustains this interpretation – indeed, when he is quizzed by the 'friar', Escalus's first description of the Duke is as 'One that, above all other strifes, contended especially to know himself' (III.2.222–3) – but it also allows for a Duke who is politically calculating and cold-blooded rather than psychologically bruised and reflective.

In the early part of the play, the Duke is concerned with abdication, with giving up his powers and with a retreat into a less active life. As the truth about Angelo's behaviour emerges, however, he becomes more and more active, spinning his complicated plans to bring about the resolution. Whereas the first half of the play could be seen to derive its energy from the encounters between Angelo and Isabella, the second half is dominated, prompted, by the Duke. His new-found activity is analogous to that of the dramatic author or director: he invents a plot and positions his characters, while enjoying superior knowledge about how events will turn out. This firmness of purpose involves a certain amount of cruelty to the participants. The Duke could have revealed himself to countermand the order to execute Claudio, but instead he delivers a long homily on life's empty pleasures and bids the hapless prisoner 'Be absolute for death' (III.1.5). He could have told Isabella that Claudio had in fact been spared, but instead his announcement that her brother is dead is abrupt and callous. He makes Mariana think that her long-awaited husband is to be executed and puts Isabella to the humiliation of begging for the life of a man at whose hands she has suffered. He even lets the Provost think he has lost his job for disobeying orders. In the last scene the other characters on stage seem puppets in the Duke's hands and only Lucio, in his audacious unmasking of the 'friar', offers a challenge to this tyranny, exercised through a combination of plotting and quick improvisation. For Roger Allam as the Duke, this last scene 'felt as if I was subjecting them, Isabella, Angelo, and Mariana, to some kind of ordeal by fire. The sequence as a whole had the ritual of purification.' Another more cynical reading might suggest that it registers the Duke's resumption of office, his sense of, and renewed enjoyment in, his own autocratic power. It is a power before which Lucio's unwitting crime of 'Slandering a prince' (V.1.521) is one of the worst of all offences.

ISABELLA

Isabella is a character who seems to demand us to understand her better than she understands herself. Her decision to enter a convent is never explained, and many critics have sought to characterise this as a running away, a desire to escape the problems and pressures of 'real life', rather than as a considered consequence of her piety. A widespread assumption that the nun's vow of chastity means that she is sexually repressed, a hotbed of seething and barely restrained passions, has affected interpretations of Isabella's character. Certainly, Isabella is not unaffected by her involvement in a plot which is preoccupied by illicit sexuality. She is the focus of the play's sexual dynamic, as Angelo finds himself almost overwhelmed with desire, and even the Duke proposes marriage to her.

She is implicated in the play's grubby sex plot, and without a qualm she engineers the bed-trick, subjecting another woman to the sexual fate she so vehemently defends herself against. Some critics have read in her language a subconscious eroticism, notably in her sensuous desire 'to strip myself to death as to a bed / That long I have been sick for' (II.4.102–3) rather than submit to Angelo. Paula Dionisotti, who played Isabella for the RSC in 1978, described her character as 'innocent, not naïve' – she is, after all, able to play the grubby game of blackmail with Angelo when she threatens 'Sign me a present pardon for my brother, / Or with an outstretched throat I'll tell the world / What man thou art' (II.4.152–4). The 1978 production used Isabella's costume to suggest 'her increasing ambivalence towards retreat' through the alterations to her habit : 'the hood came back, the sleeves got rolled up, dirt appeared at the hem'. Dionisotti added that 'my Isabella was very frightened of sexuality ... [she] doesn't particularly enjoy being among people ... because people are so complicated to deal with, and you have to deal with all their contradiction, and of course their contradictions force you to look at your own, which is what Claudio does to Isabella'. 'Isabella craves simplicity and order and certainty – her belief – but is faced with confusion and contradiction – humanity.' For another Isabella, Juliet Stevenson, who took on the role in 1983, Isabella was a much more positive character, one who 'recognises her own sensuality and the need to apply strict control over it. I don't think she's frightened or surprised by it; she wants to dominate it.' This recalls Isabella's request for 'more stricter restraint' (I.4.4) in her earliest words in the play. Both these actors' interpretations stress Isabella's need for control – of herself or of her environment – and this element of her character connects with Angelo's similar need for restraint, of himself and others.

It is in her two scenes opposite Angelo, and one with her brother, that Isabella's character expresses its energy. The play offers her little room for soliloquy: hers is a character which emerges through her interaction with others. Her only moment alone on stage is her short speech after her interview with Angelo at the end of II.4, in which she acknowledges her own isolation: 'To whom should I complain?' (II.4.171). It is at this point that she delivers the line which is perhaps most difficult for modern readers and audiences to accept, 'More than our brother is our chastity' (II.4.185). Even here, she avoids the direct, confessional first-person form of address – it is not 'more than *my* brother is *my* chastity'. This is a formal statement of belief rather than an inner revelation of feeling. Unlike Angelo, she does not seem to struggle with her conscience, but instead comes to an adamant, even extreme, certainty which many readers have found unsympathetic. But in a more religious age, life itself seemed a short and insignificant matter in the light of eternal judgement. 'Death is a fearful thing' – perhaps Claudio's terror speaks more immediately to us now, but Isabella's reply 'And shamèd life a hateful' (III.1.120–1) represents the moral orthodoxy of the time, and no-one in the play itself criticises her for this firm belief, as even Claudio repents of his attempts to persuade her otherwise. It is striking that the most fervent (or is it ironic?) appreciation of her piety comes from the irreverent Lucio, who describes her as 'a thing enskied and ensainted' (I.4.34). Her declarations of her faith, as for example, at II.2.73ff, sound a note of real conviction, particularly when compared to the sententious wisdom of the Duke (III.1.5ff). He is always a fake friar, whereas her calling is a genuine one.

Isabella's character blossoms in debate. At first she is hesitant and timorous with Angelo, but on Lucio's insistence she reveals her determined and expressive nature. Claudio's description of her 'prosperous art / When she will play with reason and discourse, / And well she can persuade' (I.2.183–5) is amply realised in the presentation of her arguments to his judge. After the emotional roller-coaster of the first scene in Act III, however, her role is less prominent – she appears tired and compliant in place of her fierce and eloquent passions in the first half of the play. Her weariness seems almost palpable by the final scene: she expresses no welcome or relief at Claudio's deliverance, and her plea for Angelo's remission is stilted and forced, particularly by contrast to her heartfelt petition for her brother's life. In her first appearance she is taken from the convent to which she wants to dedicate her life, and she never returns there. Her response to the Duke's proposal is enigmatically silent, and this is perhaps the logical conclusion of her increasingly muted presence throughout the play. Does she marry him or not? The play allows us to decide. Her silence may be interpreted as a sign of resistance to his plans, or as wordless compliance. And either of these alternatives begs further questions. Would she reject the Duke because she is repressed or frightened, as an agony aunt might put it, of commitment?

Or because she is committed to her religious vocation and has no need of a husband? Or because the Duke's undercover machinations have not endeared him to her? If she accepts him, are we to believe she is in love with him? There has been no hint of it. Is her independent spirit broken so that she acquiesces with his plan just as she went along with the bed-trick? Has this awkward, self-assured character been assimilated into a romantic conclusion, or does she remain resolved to follow her own path?

ANGELO

Much of Angelo's behaviour invites our hostility. His attempt to take advantage of Isabella's desperate concern for her brother's life, his lack of humanity in applying the law so harshly to Claudio, his abandonment of a fiancée when her dowry is lost – these actions are not designed to make him sympathetic. His personality in the play is structured between the extremes of chastity and desire, as the man whose 'urine is congealed ice' (Lucio, III.2.104) turns into 'an hypocrite, a virgin-violator' (Isabella, V.1.41). It would be easy to categorise Angelo as the moral crusader whose severity is directed at others as a smokescreen for his own desires – the early modern equivalent of the errant television evangelist or right-wing politician whose public pronouncements on sexual morality are at odds with a sleazy private life – but this is not the whole story. Certainly the impression of the public Angelo is of a man holding himself in check, whose speech is clipped and precise, and for whom self-restraint is a way of life. Even the smile which seems to have been characteristic (II.2.187, V.1.163, V.1.231) suggests a fixed, mask-like expression, keeping the emotions and reactions under control. Descriptions of him repeatedly use images which express steadfastness, even rigidity: 'a man of stricture and firm abstinence' (I.3.12) who 'scarce confesses / That his blood flows' (I.3.52), 'whose blood / Is very snow-broth' (I.4.57), 'most strait in virtue' (II.1.9), 'severe' (II.1.269). Lucio talks of him needing to be 'soften[ed]' (I.4.70), and when Claudio describes the new governor as a rider showing his control over the horse of state with his spur (I.2.1158ff), the image could also serve for Angelo's relationship to his own animal desires. This language of restraint, of passions curbed, conforms to Angelo's own appearances in the play, and it is significant that he uses the corresponding imagery of release about his sexual desires:

'now I give my sensual race the rein' (II.4.160). His repressed emotions are violently released, hot and urgent from the pressure of constraint (see Themes – Freedom & Restraint).

Angelo is a man proud of his 'unsoiled name' (II.4.154): 'yea, my gravity, / Wherein let no man hear me, I take pride' (II.4.9–10), and while this pride may be a kind of **hubris**, the play does not suggest that he is serially hypocritical. He is a man once tempted, not habitually deceitful. (Were there any hint of previous slips in Viennese gossip, we might be sure that Lucio would broadcast it.) Yet the play sometimes seems to want to make him a symbol of the gap between appearance and reality: the word 'seem' and its variants are used about him (I.3.54, II.4.150, III.1.224), and the Duke emphasises his symbolic function through a pun on Angelo's name: 'O, what may man within him hide. / Though angel on the outward side' (III.2.259–60). The psychological subtlety of Angelo's characterisation, however, resists such a black-and-white reading. It is clear that Angelo is tormented rather than gratified by his desires. His lustful feelings towards Isabella seem to be a new and involuntary experience, and suddenly he understands the libidinous drives of his fellow men. His soliloquy after his first meeting with her shows in its broken rhythms and incessant questions the tatters of his iron self-possession. He recognises his temptation and struggles with it, railing against his own desires: 'what art thou, Angelo? / Dost thou desire her foully for those things / That make her good?' (II.2.173–5), and when his behaviour is revealed, he makes no excuses, craving 'death more willingly than mercy' (V.1.473). Programme notes from a production of the play by the Cheek by Jowl company in 1994 quoted from the twentieth-century Italian poet and novelist, Cesare Pavese: 'We hate others because we hate ourselves'. Applied to Angelo, this might suggest that he punishes Claudio so harshly because he recognises, and despises, the same failings within himself. Angelo's characterisation is related to Claudio's through their parallel actions – the pre-contract between Angelo and Mariana echoes that between Claudio and Juliet, and at the end of the play Angelo's fate is seen to be dependent on Claudio's – 'An Angelo for Claudio' (V.1.406) – so that when Claudio is revealed to be alive, Angelo's life is saved (see Themes, on Symmetry & Antithesis; Substitution). Angelo's preoccupation with self-restraint also links his presentation to that of Isabella.

If Angelo's faults are manifest, there are some redeeming features. At his first appearance he seems reluctant to take on the position of deputy, seeking for 'more test' (I.1.48). If the Duke does manufacture his promotion in order to verify his suspicions of Angelo's character, as 'what our seemers be' (I.3.54) may suggest, then Angelo's fall may seem to be forced on him. His interpretation of the law is indeed severe, but then that is what is demanded of him in a situation which has deteriorated under the laxity of the Duke's regime. He tries to operate according to the letter of the law, attempting to distance his private, individual self from his public, executive position: 'It is the law, not I, condemns your brother; / Were he my kinsman, brother, or my son, / It should be thus with him' (II.2.80–2). In his soliloquies he is painfully aware of his shortcomings, although seemingly powerless to control himself. He seems to experience partial repentance for the acts he believes are on his conscience, and his preoccupation with Claudio's supposed fate is clear in his speech at the end of IV.4, in which he twice expresses 'He should have lived' (IV.4.26, 30) without naming Claudio. This speech also shows his awareness of his acts, as well as an ambivalence towards them: 'Alack, when once our grace we have forgot, / Nothing goes right. We would, and we would not' (IV.4.31–2). In the final scene he is reduced to abject humiliation and shame, and prospects for his enforced marriage to Mariana do not seem bright. 'Love her, Angelo' (V.1.523), instructs the Duke, but there is no evidence in Angelo's cold, precise, disturbed characterisation that he is capable of it.

CLAUDIO

Claudio speaks no lines at all at the end of the play. Yet at its heart, in III.1, he has a scene of extreme emotional and poetic intensity, in which some of the play's most fundamental philosophy is articulated. In a sense, Claudio is a minor character – a plot function whose presence is needed to motivate the actions and reveal the personalities of the play's major protagonists. He can be seen as a structural counterpoint to Mariana (see Themes, on Symmetry & Antithesis), another plot- rather than personality-based intervention in the play. In his one big scene, however, Claudio resists the marginalisation which has made Mariana so two-dimensional.

Other characters view Claudio with approval and affection. Mistress Overdone says to Lucio and his companions that he 'was worth five thousand of you all' (I.2.60–1), Escalus calls him a 'gentleman ' with 'a most noble father' (II.1.6–7), the Provost fervently wishes for his pardon (IV.2.68–9), Lucio declares he loved him (IV.3.155). His inherent decency is a necessary complication of the justice and punishment plot Shakespeare inherited from his sources (see Sources). The desire for restraint noted in the characters of Angelo and Isabella crops up again, more unexpectedly, in Claudio, who blames his crime on 'too much liberty' (I.2.124), for 'Our natures do pursue, / Like rats that ravin down their proper bane, / A thirsty evil, and when we drink we die' (I.2.127–9) (see Themes, on Freedom & Restraint). Claudio both accepts his failings and the justice of his arrest, and repudiates the law for his punishment, just as in prison he oscillates wildly between stoic resignation and desperate panic. He seems caught between 'stiff upper lip' and human indignation and terror. In his interview with his sister, Claudio's repeated questions demonstrate his anxious search for a remedy to his situation. While expressing his readiness for death: 'I will encounter darkness as a bride. / And hug it in mine arms' (III.1.88), his mind is still turning over the possibilities for escape: 'Sure it is no sin' (III.1.113). His speech on death has an intensity which might be expected from a tragedy, and many critics have compared it to passages in *Hamlet*, and on his heartfelt plea 'Sweet sister, let me live' audiences may find their attitude towards Isabella's stance hardening. Claudio's characterisation is economical but powerful, and his main functions are to question our judgements of other characters, especially Isabella and Angelo, and to humanise the play's discussion of abstract ideas of justice and mercy.

LUCIO

The cast-list published in the Folio describes Lucio as a 'fantastique' – one whose clothes or manners express eccentricity. Lucio's characteristic mode is rootlessness. He appears in six scenes and is a cynical, amoral character equally at home among the stews or in Angelo's apartments or in the prison. Some of the play's wittiest one-liners are given to him, as is its most severe punishment. Pompey calls him 'a gentleman' (III.2.39) and Lucio himself claims to have been an intimate of the Duke, but in fact he does not seem to fit into any single sphere or rank. His character is almost parasitic in its reliance on others: 'I am a kind of burr, I shall stick' (IV.3.175).

One of his principal functions is that of go-between. He is always going somewhere: to find out whether reports of Claudio's imprisonment are true, to seek Isabella, to Angelo. He wanders in and out of scenes, often alone. He claims 'Isabel, I loved thy brother' (IV.3.155), but will not stand bail for Pompey. Only his past liaison with Kate Keepdown suggests any kind of human contact, and his attitude towards her is crudely dismissive. In his first appearance, in I.2. he is joking about venereal disease – and this clever, cruel, edgy witticism is characteristic. When faced with Claudio's solemnity in the face of his arrest, Lucio's flippancy seems expressive of unease. He prefers 'the foppery of freedom' to 'the mortality of imprisonment' (I.2.132–3), and this disposition remains his watchword. He seems to have wriggled out of punishment and enjoys the freedom to mingle with different groups of people while his associates Claudio, Pompey and Mistress Overdone are all incarcerated. His next appearance is at the convent (I.4). In this encounter he seems to defer to Isabella's status, distinguishing his manners with her from his usual jesting dalliance with women (I.4.31–7). This is also marked by his use of the refined formality of verse speech unlike his habitual mocking prose. His account of 'your brother and his lover' (line 40) uses the imagery of natural fertility in contrast to the language of disease and commerce applied to sex elsewhere in the play. In this scene he appears an astute judge of politics and character in his descriptions of the Duke and Angelo.

In his presence at the first meeting of Isabella and Angelo in II.2 his role is to urge her on, and in the initial exchange Lucio seems to feel much more desperation and tenacity about the project than she does. His repeated 'You are too cold' (II.2.45, 56) expresses his urgency. Neither Isabella nor Angelo gives any indication of having heard him, so that his promptings seem almost disembodied. In fact it is unclear whether he is speaking audibly to Isabella or whether his observations merely form a kind of commentary on the action – certainly Lucio is a character who often seems to be speaking with an ironic awareness of the audience. As Isabella's passion and eloquence grow, his comments are admiring and supportive. His comments on the Duke are humorous and much can be made of the dramatic irony of his slanders in performance. His unwitting remarks to the 'friar' may also generate audience sympathy for him.

He seems to enjoy the power that information and gossip can give him, even if it is made up. Even to Isabella, though, his assessment of the absent Duke is equivocal 'the old fantastical Duke of dark corners' (IV.3.155–6). In the final scene he adds some welcome levity to the final scene with his constant comments – again, his is a kind of irreverent **choric** function and again he enjoys having and intervening with information, some of it false. His relation to the Duke is quite curious: his use of the word 'fantastical', recollecting the description of Lucio himself, seems to suggest a kind of equivalence between them. Both Lucio and the Duke are unattached characters and both enjoy the freedom to move between settings by which more orthodox characters would be constrained. Like the disguised Duke, Lucio is 'a looker-on here in Vienna' (V.1.315). When Lucio is accusing the disguised Duke of slandering the Duke, his scandalised interlocutor retorts 'you must, sir, change places with me, ere you make that my report' (V.1.333–4) (see Themes – Substitution). Given this characteristic slipperiness, this shiftiness, it is not surprising that Lucio considers 'marrying a punk' as 'pressing to death, whipping and hanging' (V.1.519–20) – his forcible incorporation into the social institution of marriage expresses itself as the restraint of his very being.

THEMES

SYMMETRY & ANTITHESIS

The title of the play, *Measure for Measure*, immediately introduces central idea of balance and equivalence. A common image for the process of law shows the scales of justice achieving a perfect balance, between mercy and punishment, between the severity of the crime and the severity of legal and social response. It has been suggested that Escalus's name alludes to this image, and the play also refers to it through weighing at III.2.254 and V.1.111 and in Angelo's taunt to Isabella: 'my false o'erweighs your true' (II.4.169–70). In some ways, *Measure for Measure* may be seen to seek an ideal balance, as it tries to reconcile the absolutes – the letter of the law for Angelo, chastity for Isabella, life or death for Claudio – which have motivated its characters and action. As the Duke remarks in the final scene, the law cries out for reparation: '"An Angelo for Claudio, death for death!" / Haste still pays haste, and leisure answers leisure, / Like doth quit like, and Measure still for Measure' (V.1.406–8). His words echo both the biblical injunction 'an eye for an eye, a tooth for a tooth' (Matthew 5:38), and, in their use of the play's title, seem to resound as a kind of summary for the ethics of the whole piece. But if we look more closely at the context in which these lines are spoken, the idea of a just symmetry of crime and punishment is revealed to be more complicated than the formula of 'Measure for Measure' allows. The Duke invokes a false equivalence: Angelo's life might be placed in the balance against Claudio's, except that, as the audience knows, Claudio is not dead at all. By structuring this philosophy of justice on a conditional (see Substitution) – *if* Claudio *were* dead, Angelo's life *would be* payable in response – the play undermines its pronouncement. Given that Claudio is not dead, we don't quite know how a just punishment for Angelo might look, nor for what, under law, he is to be punished.

Other instances of apparent symmetry in the play also turn out to be unbalanced or disordered. Like Claudio, Lucio has got a woman pregnant outside marriage, but Lucio proudly parades his escape from his responsibilities. Angelo's precontractual relationship with Mariana mirrors Claudio's with Juliet, but Claudio wanted to marry Juliet whereas Angelo abandons his intended bride. In having what he believes is sex outside marriage, Angelo again revisits the actions of Claudio, but whereas the latter's crime 'was mutually committed' (II.3.27), Angelo's actions are surrounded by coercion and deceit. Repetitions in the plot, by which one situation or behaviour comments, through their similarity, on another, create much of the moral ambiguity of the play. Symmetries sometimes reveal themselves as antitheses: between liberty and restraint, between justice and mercy, between chastity and fornication, between eternal and earthly life. Although these opposites are bracketed together, they represent such extremes that no compromise or balance seems possible: *Measure for Measure* tends to dramatise incompatible belief systems rather than the possibility of a middle ground.

SUBSTITUTION

The theme of substitution is closely related to that of symmetry and antithesis: often alternatives which appear to be balanced actually require the substitution of one act or person for another. The whole plot is based on substitution – the replacement of the Duke by Angelo, and there are further substitutions, most notably the substitution of Mariana for Isabella in Angelo's bed, and the substitution of the head of Ragozine for that of Claudio in the prison. This last example involves two substitutions: first the head of Barnadine is proposed, and one effect of this added complication is to focus attention on this repeated theme. Both the bed-trick and the stay of execution of Claudio work through suggesting the interchangeability of persons. One can stand for another in a given situation: one dead head is very like another, and, more disturbingly, the play needs us to accept that bedding one woman is very like bedding another (as in the proverbial expression 'all cats are grey in the dark').

There are other kinds of substitution, too. Angelo's proposition to Isabella involves the substitution of her virginity for her brother's life. The pardon for Claudio which the Duke is expecting is substituted by a confirmation of his execution, and this in turn is substituted by the superior orders of the Duke. On a linguistic level, Elbow's malapropisms mistakenly substitutes one word for another, and the inappropriateness of these verbal substitutions suggest that other substitutions are also unsatisfactory. Whipping is substituted for execution in the case of Lucio, and married life substituted for death for him and for Angelo. Perhaps Isabella substitutes the chaste and enclosed life of the convent for marriage to the Duke. The Duke himself substitutes a monk's habit for the robes of office. His final pronouncements substitute sex contained within marriage for extramarital relationships, in an attempt to substitute the nuclear family for the brothel and suburb.

When Isabella tries to persuade Angelo to be lenient, she begs him to put himself in her brother's situation, and thus to enact an imaginative self-substitution: 'If he had been as you, and you as he, / You would have slipped like him; but he, like you, / Would not have been so stern' (II.2.64–6). The emphasis on the shifting pronouns enacts, at the level of her **syntax**, the act of identification she seeks to prompt. Her plea for imaginative substitution, imagining oneself in the position of another, is also what is required of the play's audience. In order to become involved with the play's ethical questioning we need to imagine what we might do or how we might feel in the situation of the characters. This empathy shifts with the unfolding plot: one set of sympathies is substituted for another, as our responses to the characters develop. Escalus also asks Angelo to empathise with Claudio, wondering 'whether you had not sometime in your life / Erred in this point which now you censure him' (II.1.14–6). The irony in both cases is, of course, that Angelo will actually, not imaginatively, take the place of Claudio as fornicator and as prisoner awaiting execution. Isabella introduces her plea with the word 'If', a word which has a particular resonance in *Measure for Measure*. It pushes the play's philosophy into the territory of the conditional, the 'what if', and also towards a sense of bargaining, the 'if you ... then I'. Both are appropriate for a play which produces ethical dilemmas and scenarios within a structure of substitution and antithesis.

FREEDOM & RESTRAINT

One of the play's most fundamental thematic oppositions is between freedom and restraint, and as with many apparent oppositions, the distinctions between the two poles become increasingly blurred. On one level, freedom and restraint are physical states, represented by the brothel and the prison. Other physically restricted places are important to the play: Isabella wishes 'a more strict restraint' (I.4.4) in the enclosed convent of St Clare, although she never returns to it, and Mariana's 'moated grange' (III.1.265) and Angelo's 'garden circummured with brick' (IV.1.27) are both locations defined by enclosure, as indeed is Vienna itself (the Duke is to return to the city gates).

More significantly, however, these defined geographical spaces seem symbolic of inner, psychological restraint. It is entirely appropriate to Angelo's self-controlled character that he should have a walled garden (see Characterisation), and Mariana's willing immolation within her moated home shows how she has kept herself from the world since Angelo's desertion, but also how she has waited for him: 'His unjust unkindness, that in all reason should have quenched her love, hath, like an impediment in the current, made it more violent and unruly'

(III.1.241–4). These secluded and surrounded habitations may also symbolise a virginal integrity, the unbroken and unentered body of chastity. Angelo refers to this association when he muses, after Isabella's departure, 'Shall we desire to raze the sanctuary / And pitch our evils there?' (II.2.171–2). Self-control, for both Angelo and Isabella, is both a freedom and a restraint (see Characterisation).

Freedom may seem an entirely positive state, but the play associates too much freedom with the perceived laxity and debauchery of Viennese society. Paradoxically, Claudio blames 'too much liberty' (I.2.124) for his arrest, arguing that human nature is not fit to regulate its own freedom: 'Our natures do pursue / Like rats that ravin down their proper bane, / A thirsty evil, and when we drink we die' (I.2.127–9). Angelo's government is described in terms of the rider's assertion of his authority over the unruly horse (I.2.158ff), and the imagery is repeated by the Duke at I.3.19–20 (see Textual Analysis, on Text 1): Vienna is a state which needs some restraint in order to enjoy freedom. As Claudio observes, 'every scope by the immoderate use / Turns to restraint' (I.2.126–7). Elsewhere, scope or expansiveness comes to mean restraint: when Isabella tells Claudio of the unacceptable price of his freedom, she uses the same opposition in 'a restraint, / Though all the world's vastidity you had, / To a determined scope' (III.1.71–3).

Both life and death are represented in terms of freedom and restraint during the play. For Isabella, a sinful life is 'Perpetual durance' (III.1.70), freeing life but fettering the soul eternally. Claudio, on the other hand, sees death as being frozen in 'thick ribbèd ice, / To be imprisoned in the viewless winds' (III.1.126–7), despite being advised by the 'friar' that death is a release from burdensome life (III.1.4ff). At the end of the play, all the principals are released from prison or sentence, but are they, can they, and should they be, free?

CRIME, PUNISHMENT AND JUSTICE

The question of crime, punishment and justice is a major preoccupation of *Measure for Measure*. The law has swung like a pendulum from one extreme to another, from laxity to severity, and there seems to be no middle way. The Duke's final arrangement of affairs in the last act of the play begs as many questions as it answers. Many critics have felt that

Angelo ought, in fairness, to be punished (see Critical History & Broader Perspectives), although perhaps his public humiliation, his shattered self-image and his enforced marriage to Mariana are punishment enough. This apparent leniency contrasts with the threatened severity of Lucio's treatment. 'Slandering a prince' (V.1.521) appears to be the worst offence demanding the harshest penalty. For Angelo and Lucio, marriage is proposed as punishment (for men) and reward or deserts (for women), and the romantic side of marriage is tainted by this association. The pardoning of Barnadine, in whose case there are no mitigating factors and whose crime of murder far outweighs any other committed in the play, also casts doubt on the justice of the Duke's decrees. These last-act amnesties seem to bear little relation to the facts of the crimes committed.

This difficulty, of the appropriate balance between crime and punishment, runs through the play. Everything points to the unwarranted severity of Claudio's treatment, and Juliet's appearance in the play makes it clear that his behaviour is part of a consensual and committed relationship, rather than the violent acts of his prototype in the sources (see Sources) or the casual fornication of the brothel's clients. The play dramatises the difficulty of a just enforcement of the law. Angelo admits 'what knows the laws / That thieves do pass on thieves?' (II.1.22–3); Isabella maintains that only God 'is the top of judgement' (II.2.75), deferring earthly punishment. Angelo debates with Isabella and with Escalus the place of mercy or leniency in the law, sticking firmly to his view that it must not be made a 'scarecrow' on which birds perch unafraid (II.1.1), and while this is not in itself indefensible, the particular instances of its operation in the play do not foster our sympathy.

The play has a preponderance of courtroom scenes, and all these demonstrations of the legal process at work are unsatisfactory. In II.1, constable Elbow's repeated malapropisms and Pompey's timewasting speeches bring the proceedings down to a farce of unwitting puns and wordy filibustering. The matter of Elbow's wife, her pregnancy and her suspected (or is it respected? II.1.153ff) virtue entirely draw the attention away from the charges of bawding and pimping levelled at Pompey. Angelo's exasperated departure is preceded by a rare moment of wry humour – 'This will last out a night in Russia / When nights are longest there' (II.1.128–9), and Escalus is left to dispense justice. His verdict is feeble, if a pragmatic one, and Pompey's cheerful recognition that the commercial rewards of prostitution and the perennial attraction of casual sexual activity will always overrule the law casts the whole system into doubt. Nothing in the play contradicts his prediction that the law will not 'hold in Vienna ten year' (II.1.229–30), and the fact that he is arrested again in III.2 demonstrates the ineffectiveness of legal sanctions. The silence of the figure of Justice in II.1 is highly symbolic – and his only speech is to condemn Angelo rather than the malefactors (II.1.269). Even the Duke's fierce denunciation of Pompey in III.2.17ff seems to roll off its slippery target, as he continues his unrepentant jesting under the tutelage of the hangman Abhorson.

None of the play's persistent offenders seems to repent or show any hint of reformation: Barnadine, Pompey, and to some extent Lucio, show the limits of the law's power to enforce social and sexual morality in the face of such concerted criminality. There seems no reason to think that Vienna's moral crisis is over with the Duke's return to power, and nor is there any clarity about how he intends in future to avoid both the laxity of his previous regime and the severity of Angelo's interpretation of the law. The play judges the idea of justice and the conduct of those who seek to dispense it, as well as those who are on the receiving end.

IMAGERY & LANGUAGE

Measure for Measure is written in a variety of styles, from the earthy, bawdy prose of Pompey to the shortened rhyming lines of the Duke's moralising commentary. Shifts between prose and verse are important and may comment on the status of the speakers (as in the difference between Claudio's blank verse philosophy and Lucio's prose jesting in I.2), but there is no clear class-based distinction between prose and verse speakers. Many of the play's characters, including the Duke, Escalus, Isabella and Claudio, use different forms at different points. End-rhyming is often employed to suggest proverbial wisdom, and in the mouth of the disguised Duke, the device has a quality almost of incantation (it has been pointed out that the rhyming couplets at III.2.175–8 and 249–270 echo the rhythms of the witches' spells in *Macbeth*.)

In a play preoccupied by sex, it is not surprising that bawdy and innuendo are the dominant features of the language of *Measure for Measure*. For some characters and in some situations, this is conscious, as in Lucio's punning on venereal diseases in I.2, and the slick and slippery language reveals and symbolises his moral shiftiness. Such language has, however, tainted the whole play. When Isabella tells Angelo 'I am come to know your pleasure' (II.4.31), even her modesty has been subconsciously affected by the prevailing language of sexual promiscuity and availability. Elsewhere, terms are overweighted with sexual meanings: the term 'pregnant', for example, used metaphorically by the Duke at I.1.11 and Angelo at II.1.23, also contains its literal meaning, particularly when the figure of the expectant mother Juliet, 'very near her hour' (II.2.16) serves as a visual reminder of the consequences of sexual activity. In addition to the language of sex, there are some passages of extended philosophic richness in the play: Claudio on his fear of death, for example (III.1.121–135), or Isabella on the only true judgement (II.2.73–9).

In her book *Shakespeare's Imagery and What it Tells us* (Cambridge University Press, 1935), Caroline Spurgeon identifies a high incidence of **personification** in the play. Many examples of this figure involve images of the legal process, including 'liberty plucks justice by the nose' (I.3.39), 'The law hath not been dead, though it hath slept' (II.2.90) and 'The very mercy of the law cries out / Most audible, even from his proper tongue' (V.1.404–5).

TREATMENT OF TIME

As with many of Shakespeare's plays, the timescale of *Measure for Measure* seems inconsistent. For example, did the moral rot in Vienna set in nineteen years previously, as Claudio tells us (I.2.167) or only fourteen, as in the Duke's account (I.3.21)? How much time do the events of the play take? An immediate chronology can be established from indicators such as Lucio's promise to tell Isabella of Claudio's arrest 'within two hours' (I.2.192) and her response that she will bring news to her brother 'soon at night' (I.4.88). Lucio offers to 'send after the Duke' (I.2.173), suggesting that he has not been long gone. Angelo tells Isabella to attend him the next day (II.2.160), and at that second meeting he again gives her a day's grace: 'Answer me tomorrow' (II.4.167). Isabella vows to go to her brother straight after this interview, and at the end of the scene of their meeting the 'friar' sends her back to Angelo, bidding that 'If for this night he entreat you to his bed, give him promise of satisfaction' (III.1.263–4). There are numerous references to the date and time of Claudio's execution, and this appointment is apparently brought forward by Angelo's written command. The 'friar' promises the Provost that the Duke will return within 'these two days' (IV.2.192) and then tells that he 'comes home tomorrow' (IV.3.126). As the plot develops under the Duke's orchestration, events escalate into an almost unreal time-frame: the five lines given to the Duke while Isabella tells Mariana about his plot in IV.1.59–64 are far too short to allow for the information to be conveyed. Repeated injunctions to 'hurry' or 'go speedily' give an indication of the quickening pace. And yet against this feeling that the Duke's absence may have been of only a few days' duration is the evidence that he knows Mariana well in his friar's disguise: she announces his arrival with 'Here comes a man of comfort, whose advice / Hath often stilled my brawling discontent' (IV.1.8–9). Similarly, Mistress Overdone's remark that 'Kate Keepdown was with child by [Lucio] in the Duke's time' (III.2.190–1) also suggests that Angelo's vice-governorship has been rather longer.

PART FOUR

Textual analysis

TEXT 1   (I.3.19–54)

DUKE: We have strict statutes and most biting laws,
The needful bits and curbs to headstrong weeds,   20
Which for this fourteen years we have let slip;
Even like an o'ergrown lion in a cave,
That goes not out to prey. Now, as fond fathers,
Having bound up the threatening twigs of birch,
Only to stick it in their children's sight   25
For terror, not to use, in time the rod
Becomes more mocked than feared, so our decrees,
Dead to infliction, to themselves are dead,
And liberty plucks justice by the nose;
The baby beats the nurse, and quite athwart   30
Goes all decorum.

FRIAR THOMAS: It rested in your grace
To unloose this tied-up justice when you pleased,
And it in you more dreadful would have seemed
Than in Lord Angelo.

DUKE: I do fear, too dreadful.
Sith 'twas my fault to give the people scope,   35
'Twould be my tyranny to strike and gall them
For what I bid them do: for we bid this be done
When evil deeds have their permissive pass
And not the punishment. Therefore, indeed, my father,
I have on Angelo imposed the office,   40
Who may, in th'ambush of my name, strike home,
And yet my nature never in the sight
To do it slander. And to behold his sway
I will, as 'twere a brother of your order,
Visit both prince and people. Therefore, I prithee,   45
Supply me with the habit, and instruct

How I may formally in person bear me
Like a true friar. More reasons for this action
At our more leisure shall I render you;
Only this one – Lord Angelo is precise,   50
Stands at a guard with envy, scarce confesses
That his blood flows, or that his appetite
Is more to bread than stone. Hence shall we see,
If power change purpose, what our seemers be.

Exeunt

This scene gives some further information about the Duke's character
and motives in giving up his authority to Angelo, following on from the
previous scene in which Claudio is arrested, a casualty of Angelo's new
regime. In I.2, first Lucio and his friends and then Claudio discuss the
Duke's absence: here, in conversation with Friar Thomas, the Duke
appears to talk about the state of Vienna and the collapse of discipline
and respect for the law.

The Duke paints a picture of the world turned upside down because
the laws have not been enforced: 'quite athwart / Goes all decorum' (lines
30–1). He uses a sequence of animal and social imagery to convey this
disturbed state, and his first image is a mixed metaphor which may
highlight both the topsy-turvy state of Vienna and of the Duke himself.
Line 20's 'bits and curbs to headstrong weeds' begins with the imagery of
riding and controlling a horse (compare Claudio's description of Angelo's
governorship as that of a man on a new mount showing the beast who is
in control in the previous scene, I.2.158ff), and turns to the image of the
unweeded garden as a symbol of political disorder. The law has been like
an 'o-ergrown lion in a cave' (line 22) which does not go out hunting, and
the **simile** aptly conveys the picture of a once terrible and lordly beast run
to fat and indolence. The image of the baby beating the nurse (line 30)
makes another comparison with an unnatural situation as an indication of
how out of order matters have got – instead of receiving correction from
its nurse, the infant itself dispenses punishment. Through the language
of his speech of lines 19–31, the Duke stresses the irregularity of social
affairs because of the breakdown of law and order. His word 'terror' (line
26) echoes his use at I.1.19, in which the Duke seems to identify 'terror'
as the prerogative of authority. Indeed, the Duke's language is full of

violence: the lawless state he represents is a hostile and dangerous one, but then so is the law itself. His view of the law here is as a punitive instrument of corporal punishment, which contrasts with his apparent embrace of the concept of mercy in the final scene. The law ought to be 'biting' (line 19); 'threatening twigs of birch' wielded by fathers against their children; the rod ought to be 'feared' (line 27); the baby 'beats' the nurse (line 30); it would 'be my tyranny to strike and gall them' (line 36); Angelo 'may, in th'ambush of my name, strike home' (line 41).

Throughout his first speech, the Duke's imagery distances him from the events he describes. The use of the pronoun 'we' (line 19) suggests only a formal responsibility for what is happening: this is the 'we' of the public figure, the representative of the state and the law. Friar Thomas's intervention, however, switches the responsibility for the law onto the Duke personally. His mild but inescapable question asks why the Duke did not use his authority 'to unloose this tied-up justice' (line 32), and the image suggests disorder since here it is justice which is imprisoned rather than doing the imprisoning. The Duke's response is immediately in the first person: 'I do fear …' (line 34), followed by a sequence of similar pronouns in the next three lines. It is the nearest he comes to an admission of liability for the state the law is in: 'twas my fault to give the people scope' (line 35). The word 'scope', as well as the friar's suggestion that the law should be released, recalls the recurrent theme of liberty and restraint running throughout the play (see Themes). The Duke seems to draw back from his acknowledgement, however, and resume his formal, public pronoun 'for we bid this be done' (line 37), although the rest of the speech is peppered with the first-person pronouns. It could be argued that part of reason for the Duke's withdrawal from his office is psychological, and that here he is taking a first step towards freeing himself from his public role in order to investigate and develop a private self, a man who can say 'I' rather than a ruler who always declares 'we' (see Characterisation).

In this scene, Friar Thomas serves only as a pretext for the Duke's self-revelation. He does not appear anywhere else in the play, and when the Duke needs a trustworthy friar later on, one Friar Peter is found. He does, however, provide the Duke with the disguise from which he can view his subjects and his deputy during the play. The Duke asks him for the habit and for some instruction, although it seems clear that this is to be an assumed role rather than a religious vocation. The audience is let into this secret: whereas all the other characters are taken in by the disguise (although some productions and some critics argue that Lucio sees through it), the audience always has this superior knowledge. The Duke promises more reasons for his actions later on, but delivers one important clue in the last lines of the scene. His thoughts shift to Angelo, and to his outward appearances and declarations. 'Hence we shall see, / If power change purpose, what our seemers be' (lines 53–4): the end-rhyme and the positioning of these lines at the end of a scene both add emphasis to this pronouncement, which suggests that the Duke's primary purpose is to test his suspicions about Angelo's virtue and honour. The Duke, it seems, has a plan even at this early stage of the play, and the scene invites us – 'hence we shall see' – to watch the spectacle unfold and act as witnesses to this extended and hidden trial. In its suggestion of a possible gap between 'seeming' and 'being', it is a hint of what is to come, giving the Duke an aura of control and foresight as he dons his monk's robe and cowl.

TEXT 2   (II.2.28–82)

ISABELLA: Please but your honour hear me.

ANGELO: Well, what's your suit?

ISABELLA: There is a vice that most I do abhor,
And most desire should meet the blow of justice,   30
For which I would not plead, but that I must,
For which I must not plead, but that I am
At war 'twixt will and will not.

ANGELO: Well: the matter?

ISABELLA: I have a brother is condemned to die.
I do beseech you, let it be his fault,   35
And not my brother.

PROVOST: (*aside*)   Heaven give thee moving graces.

ANGELO: Condemn the fault, and not the actor of it?
Why, every fault's condemned ere it be done.
Mine were the very cipher of a function,

To fine the faults whose fine stands in record,   40
And let go by the actor.

ISABELLA: O just, but severe law!
I had a brother then; heaven keep your honour.

LUCIO: (*aside to* ISABELLA) Give't not o'er so. To him again, entreat him,
Kneel down before him, hang upon his gown;
You are too cold. If you should need a pin,   45
You could not with more tame a tongue desire it.
To him, I say.

ISABELLA: Must he needs die?

ANGELO: Maiden, no remedy.

ISABELLA: Yes, I do think that you might pardon him,
And neither heaven nor man grieve at the mercy.   50

ANGELO: I will not do't.

ISABELLA: But can you if you would?

ANGELO: Look what I will not, that I cannot do.

ISABELLA But might you do't, and do the world no wrong,
If so your heart were touched with that remorse
As mine is to him?   55

ANGELO: He's sentenced; 'tis too late.

LUCIO: (*aside to* ISABELLA)   You are too cold.

ISABELLA: Too late? Why, no. I that do speak a word
May call it back again. Well, believe this,
No ceremony that to great ones longs,
Not the king's crown, nor the deputed sword,   60
The marshal's truncheon, nor the judge's robe,
Become them with one half so good a grace
As mercy does.
If he had been as you, and you, as he,
You would have slipped like him; but he, like you,   65
Would not have been so stern.

ANGELO: Pray you be gone.

ISABELLA: I would to heaven I had your potency,
And you were Isabel; should it then be thus?
No, I would tell what 'twere to be a judge,
And what a prisoner.

LUCIO: (*aside to* ISABELLA) Ay, touch him; there's the vein. 70

ANGELO: Your brother is a forfeit of the law,
And you but waste your words.

ISABELLA: Alas, alas;
Why, all the souls that were were forfeit once,
And He that might the vantage best have took
Found out the remedy. How would you be,   75
If He, which is the top of judgement, should
But judge you as you are? O think on that,
And mercy then will breathe within your lips,
Like man new made.

ANGELO: Be you content, fair maid,
It is the law, not I, condemns your brother;   80
Were he my kinsman, brother, or my son,
It should be thus with him. He must die tomorrow.

This first meeting between Angelo and Isabella is remarkable for its use of language and rhythm to convey the intensity of the relationship which is so quickly forged between the two protagonists.

Something of the dynamic between Angelo and Isabella can be discerned simply by looking at the shape of the scene on the printed page, and in particular at the pattern of lines in which the metre, almost like the baton in a relay race, swaps between two speakers. Isabella's first two speeches leave a gap in which Angelo inserts a terse question. It is almost as if the incomplete pentameter forces Angelo to reply, leaving a measurable silence in the metre of the line which he has to fill up. Later in the scene the roles are reversed as Isabella completes Angelo's lines. When he says 'I will not do't' (line 51), the position of the words in the pentameter undermines their stated meaning: while the words themselves speak of certainty and finality, the rhythm is half-finished, leaving a space in which Isabella can – metrically must – reopen the argument. The metrical space serves to prolong the interview: although Angelo's words say that there is no room for argument over Claudio's sentence, he does not, at some level, want to dismiss her entirely. At one point he tries to evade the logic of the completed pentameter, following her half-line 'As mine is to him?' (line 55) by assertively beginning a new line: 'He's sentenced' (line 56). At another point she seems to expect some reply to her incomplete line 'As mercy does' (line 63), and when no intervention from Angelo is forthcoming, she has to take a deep breath and start another phrase. The battle between them is thus conducted through control of the language and metre of their altercation, and the ways in which their language comes together to form the pentameters of blank **verse** suggests a definite relationship between them.

The language of this extract therefore demonstrates the extent to which each is intensely aware of the other. They are circling round each other, almost dancing, locked together in the rhythms of argument and debate. Lucio's persistent injunctions to her to warm up are never directly answered or acknowledged: the pair hardly seem to notice his presence, or that of the Provost. Perhaps it is no wonder that Angelo finds the encounter so stimulating, as he reveals in his soliloquy at the end of the scene: the back-and-forth of their exchange has a kind of sensuous energy. Juliet Stevenson, who played Isabella at the RSC in 1983, has described the language in this scene as 'erotic', suggesting '[Isabella] and Angelo have been copulating across the verse ever since they met' (see Critical History & Broader Perspectives). How far Isabella is aware of this sexual current is a question for performance (see Characterisation).

As well as the erotics of the encounter, this scene dramatises some of the extremes of the play's ethical framework. At first, Angelo tries to hide behind a formal, impersonal concept of the law. He replies to 'Must he needs die?' with the bland 'Maiden, no remedy' (line 48), but Isabella wrong-foots him into taking responsibility for the decision. By introducing the insistent first-person: 'I do think that you might pardon him', Isabella puts the onus on Angelo, the man standing before her, rather than on some abstracted and intangible legal function, and he responds: 'I will not do't' (line 51). It is an unwilling concession by which Angelo acknowledges that he is personally responsible, and Isabella uses this as a weakened point in his resistance, seizing on the possibility of working a further concession. Her prime weapon is the emotive figure of substitution (see Themes, on Substitution): she repeatedly invites, even

Text 2 continued

demands, that Angelo see the situation from different viewpoints, that he imagine himself in a different role: 'If he had been as you, and you as he' (line 64); 'I would to heaven I had your potency, / And you were Isabel' (lines 67–8); 'How would you be, / If He, which is the top of judgement, should / But judge you as you are?' (lines 75–7). Angelo tries to reinstate some distance between his private person and his public position: 'It is the law, not I, condemns your brother' (line 80): like the Duke in I.3 (see Text 1), he is hesitant around his personal responsibility, preferring to present the law as separate and autonomous.

Isabella also works on Angelo by taking up his words and giving them new meanings. She turns his terms of earthly justice, that Claudio 'is a forfeit of the law' (line 71), and ups the moral stakes by transforming them into spiritual ones: 'all the souls that were were forfeit once' (line 73), so that the repetition of the word makes Claudio and Angelo equal with all the rest of sinful humanity. She presents the case for mercy as the prerequisite of the great ruler. After a shaky start – her 'let it be his fault, / And not my brother' (lines 35–6) is awkwardly phrased, and it seems that Angelo will be able to brush her off without difficulty. His rhetorical question (line 37) exposes the weakness of her opening salvo, and she is ready to give up. Urged on by Lucio, however, her arguments gain in eloquence and passion: Angelo has relatively little to say for himself in this early part of their encounter. What is clear, however, is the erotic and philosophic concentration of their meeting, as the scene continues to dramatise a relationship which creates a palpable electric energy.

TEXT 3   (III.2.57–88)

CLAUDIO: Now, sister, what's the comfort?

ISABELLA: Why,
As all comforts are: most good, most good indeed.
Lord Angelo, having affairs to heaven,   60
Intends you for his swift ambassador,
Where you shall be an everlasting leiger.
Therefore your best appointment make with speed;
Tomorrow you set on.

CLAUDIO: Is there no remedy?

ISABELLA: None, but such remedy as, to save a head,   65
To cleave a heart in twain.

CLAUDIO: But is there any?

ISABELLA: Yes, brother, you may live;
There is a devilish mercy in the judge,
If you'll implore it, that will free your life,
But fetter you till death.

CLAUDIO: Perpetual durance?   70

ISABELLA: Ay, just. Perpetual durance, a restraint,
Though all the world's vastidity you had,
To a determined scope.

CLAUDIO: But in what nature?

ISABELLA: In such a one as, you consenting to't,
Would bark your honour from that trunk you bear,   75
And leave you naked.

CLAUDIO: Let me know the point.

ISABELLA: O, I do fear thee, Claudio, and I quake
Lest thou a feverous life shouldst entertain,
And six or seven winters more respect
Than a perpetual honour. Dar'st thou die?   80
The sense of death is most in apprehension,
And the poor beetle that we tread upon
In corporal sufferance finds a pang as great
As when a giant dies.

CLAUDIO: Why give you me this shame?
Think you I can a resolution fetch   85
From flowery tenderness? If I must die,
I will encounter darkness as a bride,
And hug it in mine arms.

When Claudio was arrested in Act I, his sister Isabella occurs to him as the only possibility of helping his situation. He tells Lucio that he has 'great hope' (I.2.181) in her powers of persuading Angelo, and Lucio replies 'I pray she may' (line 186). Isabella herself is confident that she will succeed, sending Lucio with a message back to Claudio, promising 'Soon at night / I'll send him certain word of my success' (I.4.89). When she has refused Angelo's sexual bargain, she assures herself in her only soliloquy that Claudio would rather die twenty times over than suffer her to experience 'such abhorred pollution' (II.4.183). She will break the news to him and 'fit his mind for death, for his soul's rest' (II.4.188). All this, plus Claudio's own interview with the disguised Duke and his resignation around death at the beginning of III.1, serves to build up the tension around the first meeting of brother and sister: this is the scene when she has to confess her failure – some might call it her unwillingness – to save him. How will each respond to the other?

The Duke and the Provost withdraw: Claudio is eager for news, 'what's the comfort?' (III.1.57). Despite his expressed readiness for death after the Duke's long homily (III.1.5ff), he is clearly desperate for an escape. Isabella's 'Well' (line 58) is a word alone on a line. It is possible to imagine her steeling herself in that pause, taking a deep breath, to tell her unwelcome news, and this long hesitation created by the lineation may also suggest that she is not quite so sure of Claudio's reactions as she professed herself at the end of II.4. She uses a technique identifiable in her interview with Angelo in the previous scene (see Text 2): picking up 'comfort' (line 57), to which Claudio gives an immediate, earthly meaning, and transforming it into the religious idea of comfort in heaven after death. Claudio takes 'Perpetual durance' (line 70) to mean the commutation of his sentence from execution to life imprisonment; for Isabella the words mean the eternal imprisonment of the sinful soul or the stained conscience. It is noticeable that whereas the Duke's speech on death was entirely without an idea of Christian salvation, Isabella's view of death is entirely conditioned by her religious convictions. Death for her is therefore a very different prospect.

Isabella's delivery of her news is circumlocutory: she uses the image of Claudio as an ambassador going to heaven as if it were another court, preparing the way for his ruler. His 'Is there no remedy?' (line 64) precisely echoes Angelo's 'no remedy' at II.2.48, and he breaks in on Isabella's religious approach to his fate with an urgent question. This desperate questioning recurs at lines 66, 70, 73 and 84: Claudio is unable to accept the finality of his fate, perhaps because Isabella admits that there is, in fact, a remedy, albeit one that would 'cleave a heart in twain' (line 66). Her obfuscation, perhaps born of fear about his reaction, gives him space to hope, and he worries away at her more poetic, obscure diction with terse interrogatives. This space for hope is literally present in her unfinished pentameters, which leave a metrical gap for him to fill (see also Text 2). She is able to interpret his response: 'I do fear thee' (line 77). Isabella's language is full of rather formal words: Shakespeare does not use 'leiger' (line 62) or 'vastidity' (line 72) anywhere else, and 'durance' (line 70) is also a rarity. These unfamiliar, carefully chosen words convey a kind of stiffness, even coldness, about Isabella, as if they are from a speech she has prepared (compare Angelo's 'prolixious' at II.4.162, or Isabella's 'prompture' at II.4.178, neither of which occurs anywhere else in Shakespeare). Claudio castigates her use of language: 'Think you I can a resolution fetch / From flowery tenderness?' (lines 85–6). Only action, not talk, can ameliorate the situation.

At the centre of the play, III.1 is a scene of contrasting philosophies and emotions, from Claudio's stoicism to his desperate fear of death, from Isabella's tentative explanation to her anger and hurt, from the 'friar's' long speech on the worthlessness of life to the Duke's prose plottings and intrigues. This extract contains, on a smaller scale, something of the same conflict. Isabella's language is focused on heaven and on the spirituality of eternal life; Claudio's is on the immediacy of his predicament. She balances life against death, a 'head' against a 'heart (lines 65–6), freedom against fetters (lines 69–70), 'restraint' against 'scope' (lines 71–3). Isabella's attempts at comfort are sometimes unwittingly tactless: the image of the beetle's suffering in death compared to a giant's (lines 82–4) seems to stress rather than diminish 'corporal sufferance' through comparison. Isabella's argument rests on her perspective that there is 'a fate worse than death' – a tainted and sinful life; for Claudio the imminence of his execution means that his concerns are more earthly and physical. Even his imagery of death is sexualised, made physical. He is not comforted by her vision of heavenly consolation, rather he sees 'darkness as a bride' he will 'hug' to himself. This imagery links his fate to its cause, his crime of fornication. Claudio's responses to Isabella's disclosure about her dealings with Angelo prepare the audience for his pleas with his sister later in the scene.

PART FIVE

BACKGROUND

SHAKESPEARE'S LIFE

There are no personal records of Shakespeare's life. Official documents and occasional references to him by contemporaries enable us to draw the main outline of his public life, but his private life remains hidden. Although not at all unusual for a writer of his time, this lack of first-hand evidence has tempted many to read his plays as personal records and to look in them for clues to Shakespeare's own character and convictions. The results are unconvincing, partly because Renaissance art was not subjective or designed primarily to express the creator's personality, and partly because the drama of any period is very difficult to read biographically. Except when plays are written by committed dramatists to promote social or political causes (as by Shaw or Brecht), it is all but impossible to decide who amongst the variety of fictional characters in a drama represents the dramatist, or which of the various and often conflicting points of view expressed is authorial. *Measure for Measure*'s insistence on raising questions and dramatising opposing viewpoints makes any attempt to deduce Shakespeare's own feelings about his subject matter hopeless.

What we do know about Shakespeare's life can be quickly summarised. Shakespeare was born into a well-to-do family in the market town of Stratford-upon-Avon in Warwickshire in 1564, and was baptised in the town's Holy Trinity Church on 26 April. His father, John Shakespeare, was a prosperous glover and leather merchant who became a person of some importance in the town: in 1565 he was elected an alderman and in 1568 he became high bailiff, or mayor of Stratford. He married Mary Arden in 1557, and William was the third of their eight children and their eldest son. It seems probable that William went to the local grammar school where he, like all Elizabethan schoolboys, would have studied a curriculum of Latin, history, logic and rhetoric. In November 1582, when he was aged eighteen, William married Anne Hathaway, who was twenty-six. The birth of their first daughter, Susanna, six months later in May 1983, suggests either that the couple married in haste when they learned of Anne's pregnancy or that there was some kind of civil contract before the marriage ceremony. Either situation may remind us of that of Claudio and Juliet at the beginning of *Measure for Measure*. Twins, Hamnet and Judith, were born to the marriage in 1585.

Shakespeare next appears in the historical record in 1592 when he is mentioned as a London actor and playwright by the dramatist Robert Greene. These 'lost years' 1585–92 have been the subject of much speculation, but how they were occupied remains as much of a mystery as when Shakespeare left Stratford and why. In his pamphlet, *Greene's Groatsworth of Wit*, Greene expresses to his fellow dramatists his outrage that the 'upstart crow' Shakespeare has the impudence to believe he 'is as well able to bombast out a blank verse as the best of you'. To have aroused this hostility from a rival, Shakespeare must, by 1592, have been long enough in London to have made a name for himself as a playwright. We may conjecture that he had left Stratford in 1586 or 1587.

During the next twenty years, Shakespeare continued to live in London, presumably visiting his wife and family in Stratford. He continued to act, but his chief fame was as a dramatist. From 1594 he wrote exclusively for the Lord Chamberlain's Men which rapidly became the leading dramatic company and from 1603 enjoyed to patronage of James I as the King's Men. His plays were popular and he became a shareholder in the profitable theatre company, earning enough money to buy land and a large house in Stratford. He retired to his home town in about 1611, and died there on 23 April 1616. He was buried in Holy Trinity Church.

SHAKESPEARE'S DRAMATIC CAREER

Between the late 1580s and 1613 Shakespeare wrote thirty-seven plays and contributed to some by other dramatists. This was by no means an exceptional number for a professional playwright of the times, particularly in the context of a theatre industry which was hungry for new plays, each of which would probably have fewer than ten performances. The exact date of the composition of individual plays is a matter of debate – for only a few plays is the date of their first performance known – but the broad outlines of Shakespeare's dramatic career have been established. He began in the late 1580s and early 1590s with comedies, such as *The Comedy of Errors* which was heavily dependent on its source, the Latin playwright Plautus, with plays based on English history and the Wars of the Roses (*Henry VI* parts 1, 2 and 3, and *Richard III*), and with the bloodthirsty revenge tragedy *Titus Andronicus*. During the 1590s Shakespeare developed his expertise in comedies, writing plays such as *A Midsummer Night's Dream* and *As You Like It*, and produced further plays on medieval English history including *Henry IV* and *Henry V*.

As the new century begins a new note is detectable. Plays such as *Troilus and Cressida* and *Measure for Measure*, sometimes designated 'problem plays' as they poise between comedy and tragedy, evoke complex responses. These plays offer a chronological and generic bridge between the comic period of the 1590s and Shakespeare's tragedies, including *Othello*, *King Lear*, *Macbeth*, *Coriolanus* and *Antony and Cleopatra*, all written in the first decade of the seventeenth century. In the last years of his dramatic career, Shakespeare produced a group of plays often called 'romances'. These plays – *The Tempest*, *Cymbeline* and *The Winter's Tale* reprise many of the situations and themes of the earlier dramas but in fantastical and exotic dramatic designs which, set in distant lands, covering large tracts of time and involving music, mime, dance and tableaux, have something of the qualities of masques and pageants.

THE TEXTS OF SHAKESPEARE'S PLAYS

None of Shakespeare's plays exists in the author's manuscript. Nineteen were printed (not *Measure for Measure*) during his lifetime in small, cheap books called **quartos**. Shakespeare, however, did not supervise the publication of these plays. This was not unusual. When a playwright had sold a play to a dramatic company he sold his rights in it: copyright, in as much as it existed at this time, belonged to whoever had possession of an actual copy of the text, and so consequently authors had no control over what happened to their work. Several of the quartos do not even mention Shakespeare's name on their title-pages. Unlike the case of a modern author who would prepare his or her work carefully for publication and would receive proof-copies to check for printing errors before the work was circulated, Elizabethan and Jacobean dramatic texts found their way into print in various non-authorial ways. Sometimes an actor's copy of the script, or a prompt copy, perhaps cut or altered for performance, was the basis of the printed text; other quartos seem to derive from an actor or audience member's memory of the play. Printers introduced their own errors, through misreading or making their own 'corrections' where they considered it necessary. Some play-texts, for example the earliest publication of Shakespeare's *Richard II*, also show the marks of censorship.

In 1623, eight years after Shakespeare's death, John Heminges and Henry Condell, two of his fellow actors, collected together texts of thirty-six of his plays (*Pericles* was omitted) and published them together in a large book known as the First Folio. There were later editions in 1632, 1663 and 1685. Heminges and Condell promised their readers that these were the texts as Shakespeare had intended them, but this may have been a marketing ploy rather like those modern films which are remarketed as 'the director's cut' despite being essentially the same product as was already available. Despite its appearance and their assurances of its authority, however, the texts in the First Folio still present many difficulties, for there are printing errors and confused passages in the plays, and its texts often differ significantly from those of the earlier quartos, when these exist.

In the case of the text of *Measure for Measure*, the play was first published in the First Folio. There are a number of passages and phrases which have been the subject of intense labour by bibliographers, textual critics and editors. Most modern editions give an abbreviated account of the Folio text (sometimes denoted simply as F) alongside their modernised and emended version, either as a section of collation between the text and the explanatory notes (as in the Arden and World's Classics editions) or as an appendix (as in the Penguin edition). So, for example, the Penguin editor J.M. Nosworthy list over eighty alterations he has made to the Folio text, such as the substitution of 'metal' for the Folio's 'mettle' (I.1.48), the insertion of the word 'back' in the Folio's phrase 'call it again' (II.1.58), and the emendation of the Folio's troublesome word 'prenzie' in one instance to 'precise' and in another to 'precious' (III.1.97, 100). The edition also includes numerous additional stage directions, which are often very sparse in early texts.

Shakespeare's texts have, then, been through a number of intermediaries, both in his period and in our own. We do not have his authority for any one of his plays, and hence we cannot know exactly what it was that he wrote. Bibliographers, textual critics and editors have spent a great deal of effort on endeavouring to get behind the apparent errors, uncertainties and contradictions in the available texts to recover the plays as Shakespeare originally wrote them. What we read is the result of these efforts. Modern texts are what editors have constructed from the available evidence: they correspond to no sixteenth- or seventeenth-century editions, and to no early performance of a Shakespeare play. Furthermore, these composite texts differ from each other, for different editors read the early texts differently, perceive different problems and then come to different conclusions. A Shakespeare text is an unstable and a contrived thing.

Often, of course, its judgements embody, if not the personal prejudices of the editor, then the cultural preferences of the time in which he or she was working, Growing awareness of this has led recent scholars to distrust the whole editorial enterprise, and to repudiate the attempt to construct a 'perfect' text. Stanley Wells and Gary Taylor, the editors of the Oxford edition of *The Complete Works* (1986), point out that almost certainly the texts of Shakespeare's plays were altered in performance, and from one performance to another, so that there may never have been a single version. They note, too, that Shakespeare probably revised and rewrote some plays. They do not claim to print a definitive text of any play, but prefer what seems to them the 'more theatrical' version, and when there is a great difference between available versions, as with *King Lear*, they print two texts.

SHAKESPEARE & THE ENGLISH RENAISSANCE

Shakespeare arrived in London at the very time that the Elizabethan period was poised to become the 'golden age' of English Literature. Although Elizabeth reigned as queen from 1558 to 1603, the term 'Elizabethan' is used very loosely in a literary sense to refer to the period 1580 to 1625 when the great works of the age were produced. (Sometimes the later part of this period is distinguished as 'Jacobean', from the Latin form of the name of Elizabeth's successor, James VI of Scotland and I of England, who reigned from 1603 to 1625.) The poet Edmund Spenser heralded this new literary age with his pastoral poem *The Shepheardes Calender* (1579), and in his essay *An Apologie for Poetrie* (written in about 1580 and published in 1595), his patron Sir Philip Sidney championed the imaginative power of the 'speaking picture of poetry', famously declaring that 'Nature never set forth the earth in so rich a tapestry as divers poets have done ... Her world is brazen, the poets only deliver a golden'.

Spenser and Sidney were part of that rejuvenating movement in European culture which since the nineteenth century has been known by the term *Renaissance*. Meaning literally 'rebirth' it denotes a revival and redirection of artistic and intellectual endeavour which began in Italy in the fourteenth century and reached England in the early sixteenth century. Its keynote was a curiosity in thought which challenged the old assumptions and traditions: as the poet John Donne was to put it in 'An Anatomy of the World' published in 1633, 'new Philosophy calls all in doubt'. To the innovative spirit of the Renaissance, the preceding ages appeared dully unoriginal and conformist.

That spirit was fuelled by the rediscovery of many classical texts and the culture of ancient Greece and Rome. This fostered a confidence in human reason and in human potential which, in every sphere, challenged old convictions. The discovery of America and its peoples (Columbus had sailed in 1492) demonstrated that the world was a larger and stranger place than had been thought. The cosmological speculation of Copernicus (later confirmed by Galileo) that the sun, not the earth, was the centre of the planetary system challenged the centuries-old belief that the earth and human beings were at the centre of the universe. The pragmatic political philosophy of Machiavelli seemed to cut politics free from its traditional link with morality, by advising statesmen to use any means to secure a desired end. And the religious movements we know collectively as the Reformation broke with the Roman Catholic church and set the individual conscience, not ecclesiastical authority, at the centre of religious life. Nothing, it seemed, was beyond questioning, nothing impossible, although the fate of the hero of Marlowe's play *Dr Faustus* showed the limits and dangers of such radical freedom. The term 'Renaissance' suggests that this age defined itself in relation to the past.

Some historians and literary scholars have preferred to use a term which stresses the period's relationship to the future: 'early modern'. Whereas the idea of the Renaissance focuses intellectual and artistic developments, the early modern period stresses those features of life more familiar to us now: changing ideas of society, of family, of sexuality and the roles of men and women, the operations of class or rank, urban life, economics and questions of personal and cultural identity.

In its innovative and challenging stance, Shakespeare's drama is a product of its age, as well as of its creator. It interrogates (examines and asks questions of) the beliefs, assumptions and politics upon which Elizabethan society was founded. And although the plays often conclude in a restoration of order and stability, many critics are inclined to argue that their imaginative energy goes into subverting, rather than reinforcing, traditional values. *Measure for Measure* is a key illustration of Shakespearean drama's preference for active questions rather than unthinking compliance, with the authority of the play delegated to the individual members of the audience rather than centralised in a dogmatic author.

SHAKESPEARE'S THEATRE

The theatre for which Shakespeare wrote his plays was a distinctly Elizabethan invention. There had been no theatres or acting companies during the medieval period, when plays – usually on religious subjects – were performed by travelling groups of players in market-places, inn yards, and in the halls of great houses. Such actors were regarded by the authorities as little better than vagabonds and layabouts.

In the late sixteenth century, circumstances coincided to transform this situation. One influence was intellectual. A number of young men who had been to the universities of Oxford and Cambridge came to London in the 1580s and began to write plays based on their knowledge of classical dramas of ancient Greece and Rome. John Lyly, Christopher Marlowe and Thomas Kyd wrote full-length plays on secular subjects, offering a range of characterisation and situation hitherto unattempted in English drama. Lyly wrote in prose, but the other playwrights composed in the unrhymed iambic pentameters (blank verse) which the Earl of

Surrey had introduced into English earlier in the sixteenth century. This was a freer and more expressive medium than the rhymed verse of medieval drama.

Another influence on the establishment of a professional theatre was a new law forbidding travelling players unless they were under the patronage of a nobleman. (Shakespeare's company was under the patronage of the Lord Chamberlain.) This ensured that only the best troupes survived, and that their activity centred on London, where their patrons attended the queen at court. In 1576 the entrepreneur James Burbage built the first permanent playhouse, called 'The Theatre', in Shoreditch just beyond London's northern boundary. Other theatre buildings followed, mostly just outside the city walls or on the south bank of the river Thames to avoid the regulations of London's civic authorities. The theatre was not the middle-class, respectable institution of modern times: it was associated with prostitution, pickpocketing and with the spread of Plague. It was blamed for encouraging idleness and criminality, and some extreme preachers argued that the whole system of acting was a form of lying and therefore of sin. Local residents complained about the numbers of people who congregated at the theatre, and, when carriages became popular in the Jacobean period, the congestion on London Bridge caused by playgoers prompted the first parking regulations.

Shakespeare's company performed at Burbage's Theatre until 1596, and also used the Swan and Curtain theatres until moving into their own new building, the Globe, in 1599. It was burned down in 1613 when the thatched roof was ignited by a spark from a cannon fired during a performance of Shakespeare's *Henry VIII*. The Globe theatre has recently been reconstructed, using the available evidence, on Bankside, which offers some sense of the experience of theatregoing for Shakespeare's audiences.

The form of the Elizabethan theatre derived from the inn-yards and animal baiting rings which provided other kinds of entertainment. They were circular wooden buildings with a paved courtyard in the middle open to the sky. A rectangular stage jutted out into the yard, or pit, where some audience members paid a penny to stand and watch the play. Round the perimeter of the yard were tiered galleries, covered with thatch, providing more expensive seats for wealthier spectators. Performances took place in the afternoons to make use of daylight. The

THE GLOBE THEATRE,

On the Bankside.

As it appeared in the reign of King James I.

A CONJECTURAL RECONSTRUCTION OF THE INTERIOR OF THE GLOBE PLAYHOUSE

AA Main entrance
B   The Yard
CC Entrances to lowest galleries
D   Entrance to staircase and upper galleries
E   Corridor serving the different sections of
     the middle gallery
F   Middle gallery ('Twopenny Rooms')
G   'Gentlemen's Rooms or Lords Rooms'
H   The stage
J   The hanging being put up round the stage
K   The 'Hell' under the stage
L   The stage trap, leading down to the Hell
MM Stage doors

N   Curtained 'place behind the stage'
O   Gallery above the stage, used as required
     sometimes by musicians, sometimes
     by spectators, and often as part of the
     play
P   Back-stage area (the tiring-house)
Q   Tiring-house door
R   Dressing-rooms
S   Wardrobe and storage
T   The hut housing the machine for lowering
     enthroned gods, etc., to the stage
U   The 'Heavens'
W   Hoisting the playhouse flag

yard was about 80ft (24m.) in diameter, and the stage measured about
40ft (12m.) by 30ft (9m.) at 5ft (1.67m.) high, and the theatre could hold
about 3,000 spectators. The stage itself was partially covered by a roof or
canopy which projected from the wall at the rear of the stage and was
supported by two posts at the front. Two doors at the back of the stage
led into the dressing room (or 'tiring house') and it was by means of these
doors that actors entered and left the stage. Between the doors was a
small recess or alcove which was curtained off to provide a 'discovery
space', and over the discovery space was a balcony. In the early years of
the seventeenth century, Shakespeare's company acquired a smaller
indoor theatre called Blackfriars which could seat about 700 people. As a
more expensive venue, this theatre probably catered to an audience of a
higher social rank. Blackfriars had facilities for more elaborate stage
effects, including a machine for lowering actors from above the stage, and
these new possibilities were incorporated in Shakespeare's late plays.

There was little in the way of large-scale scenery, which is why
Shakespeare's characters often tell us at great length where they are or
what their surroundings are like or that it is dark or dawn or stormy. As
locations were not represented visually, they have more power as symbolic
places, perhaps suggesting an inner landscape or psychological state
rather than a specific geographical place. Props and costumes were
probably also limited. All the roles, including women, were played by
male actors. These factors, together with the form of the playhouse,
meant that audiences were always aware that they were watching a play.
The drama of the period often draws explicit attention to itself *as* drama,
using non-naturalistic conventions such as soliloquy, the imagery of
theatrical performance, or by exploring issues of disguise, role-playing,
and the gap between appearance and reality.

The early modern theatre was not concerned to make its audience
believe what it was watching was really happening – the recognition of
the artificiality of the spectacle was key to the theatrical experience.
Modern theatres, by contrast, use lighting and conventions of audience
behaviour to encourage spectators to forget themselves as they become
absorbed by the action on stage. The auditorium is usually dark, with
a passive, silent, and attentive audience watching a spotlight stage
where actors are vocal, demonstrative and dramatic. By all accounts,
Shakespeare's theatre was quite different. Audience members went to be

seen as much as to see, they were lit by natural light like the actors and wore the same kind of clothing. They had none of our modern deference, arriving late, talking and heckling during the performance, eating, drinking and conducting business. It was all much more like our experience of pantomime, where the artificiality of its conventions are enjoyed, expected and understood. But calling a theatre 'the Globe' suggests that it is a microcosm of the world, and the theatre did provide Elizabethan culture with a metaphor for understanding its own existence, as in Shakespeare's own famous observation 'All the world's a stage' (*As You Like It*). This philosophy is elaborated in a short poem by Sir Walter Raleigh:

> What is our life? The play of passion.
> Our mirth? The music of division:
> Our mothers' wombs the tiring-houses be,
> Where we are dressed for life's short comedy.
> The earth the stage; Heaven the spectator is,
> Who sits and views whosoe'er doth act amiss.
> The graves which hide us from the scorching sun
> Are like drawn curtains when the play is done.
> Thus playing post we to our latest rest,
> And then we die in earnest, not in jest.

LITERARY BACKGROUND

SOURCES

A popular moral tale current in Shakespeare's day provides the plot of *Measure for Measure*. It exists in various forms which share a basic outline. A beautiful woman goes to an official to plead for a pardon for her husband, languishing in prison under sentence of death. The official offers the pardon if she will spend the night with him. The wife agrees, reluctantly, and after she has fulfilled her part of the bargain, the official orders the execution of her husband. She complains of this treatment to some higher authority, a lord or duke, who punishes the official by forcing him to marry her, endow her with his property, and then executes him for his treachery. Many versions of the story presented it as a

Protestant morality in which the duke or lord represented a supreme wisdom, but others see his enactment of justice as unduly severe.

One version of the story known by Shakespeare was that by the Italian Giovanni Giraldi Cinthio, first published in 1565. (Shakespeare also used a plot from Cinthio's collection of stories *Hecatommithi* for *Othello*.) In Cinthio's telling of this tale, the woman is sister, not wife, to the condemned man, and her beauty and intelligence make her the central character in the narrative. Her brother is sixteen years old and in prison for rape – a crime punishable by death even though he expresses himself willing to marry his victim. The official, by contrast, has no intention of marrying the woman, seeing instead only the possibility of gratifying his own lusts. When the story emerges, he is condemned to marry her, and then she successfully pleads for his life.

This outline of Cinthio's narrative shows how Shakespeare departed from his source in certain key ways. One is his softening of the crime for which Claudio is imprisoned – the mutual act of extra-marital sex rather than the coercive violence of rape. Another is his elaboration of Isabella's chaste instincts by giving her a religious vocation, and his decision to allow her to retain her chastity through the device of the bed-trick. Cinthio's story was the source for a probably unperformed play by George Whetstone, *Promos and Cassandra* (1578), also used by Shakespeare in writing *Measure for Measure*. Whetstone adds a comic, lowlife subplot which may well have inspired Shakespeare, and he also allows the condemned brother to escape execution through the substitution of a head of another executed prisoner. In Whetstone's version it is not quite clear whether the brother's crime was consensual, as in *Measure for Measure*, or violent, as in *Hecatommithi*, but he, like Claudio, is sentenced under the provisions of an old law which has been allowed to lapse.

In collating and elaborating these versions of the existing story, Shakespeare seems to have had certain distinct purposes. First, he interrelates the different elements of the plot largely through introducing symmetries: parallels between the Duke and Angelo, Angelo and Claudio, Claudio and Isabella, Isabella and Mariana (see Themes, on Symmetry & Antithesis). Secondly he extends the role of the Duke by making him the unseen observer of events, rather than, as in Whetstone's play, a *deus ex machina* figure who makes a ceremonial and authoritative entry to dispense justice at the end of the play. Thirdly he makes moral questions central to his drama. In *Measure for Measure* more than in any of Shakespeare's sources we are required to think about the issues raised and we also need to be prepared to shift our sympathies from one character to another.

Other elements of *Measure for Measure* may have their genesis in different kinds of texts. Shakespeare seems to have borrowed from himself for the bed-trick – the substitution (see Themes, on Substitution) of Mariana for Isabella in Angelo's bed – as this device also occurs in his *All's Well that Ends Well*. There are significant biblical sources too: the play's title echoes the Sermon on the Mount. In the account in Matthew's gospel, Jesus tells his followers 'Judge not, that ye be not judged. For with what judgement ye judge, ye shall be judged; and with what measure ye mete, it shall be measured to you again' (Matthew 7:1–2). Christ warns against judging others harshly without looking at one's own faults: 'Thou hypocrite, first cast out the beam out of thine own eye; and then thou shalt see clearly to cast out the mote out of thy brother's eye' (7:5). The version in Luke's gospel urges Christians: 'Be ye therefore merciful, as your Father also is merciful. Judge not, and ye shall not be judged: condemn not, and ye shall not be condemned: forgive, and ye shall be forgiven. Give, and it shall be given unto you; good measure, pressed down, and shaken together, and running over, shall men give into your bosom. For with the same measure that ye mete withal it shall be measured to you again' (Luke 5:36–8).

PART SIX

CRITICAL HISTORY & BROADER PERSPECTIVES

EARLY RECEPTION

The earliest critics of *Measure for Measure* were somewhat nonplussed by this strange and powerful play: some were even offended or embarrassed by its frank depiction of illicit and coercive sexuality. Writing in the mid eighteenth century, Samuel Johnson considered that 'there is perhaps not one of Shakespear's plays more darkened than this by the peculiarities of its Authour', and that 'the plot is rather intricate than artful'. He also felt unhappy about the final judgement on Angelo: 'Angelo's crimes were such, as must sufficiently justify punishment ... and I believe every reader feels some indignation when he finds him spared.' A century later, the poet Samuel Taylor Coleridge went further, calling *Measure for Measure* 'a hateful work' and 'the single exception to the delightfulness of Shakspeare's plays'. Agreeing with Johnson on the morally unsatisfactory ending, Coleridge elaborated that 'our feelings of justice are grossly wounded in Angelo's escape. Isabella herself contrives to be unamiable, and Claudio is detestable.'

NINETEENTH-CENTURY CRITICISM

William Hazlitt, in his study *Characters of Shakespeare's Plays* (1817) was more favourable to the play, describing it 'as full of genius as it is of wisdom'. Like Coleridge, however, Hazlitt also found the main protagonists dislikeable, judging that 'there is, in general a want of passion; the affections are at a stand; our sympathies are repulsed and defeated in all directions'. Hazlitt identifies 'a general system of cross-purposes between the feelings of the different characters and the sympathy of the reader or audience', as he finds the Duke 'more absorbed in his own plots and gravity than anxious for the welfare of the state' and Isabella's 'rigid chastity' unappealing. For Hazlitt, the play's predominant 'principle of repugnance' reaches its height in the defiantly amoral character of Barnadine. Another expression of dissatisfaction with the play's resolution is found in the poet A.C. Swinburne's *A Study of Shakespeare* first published in 1879. Swinburne describes the audience's feelings: 'we are left hungry and thirsty after having been made to thirst and hunger for some wholesome single grain at least of righteous and too long retarded retribution: we are tricked out of our dole, defeated of our due, lured and led on to look for some equitable and satisfying upshot, defrauded and derided and sent empty away'. In his reading, the play 'is in its very inmost essence a tragedy', but its 'elaborate machinery' of plot and its ingenuity are morally unworthy of Shakespeare's genius.

A late nineteenth-century perspective from Walter Pater gives a more positive assessment of the play. Pater considered the quality of *Measure for Measure* to be variable, but that this inconsistency might account for 'some of that depth and weightiness which makes this play so impressive, as with the true seal of experience, like a fragment of life itself, rough and disjointed indeed, but forced to yield in places its profounder meaning'. The play is, above all, 'indicative ... of Shakespeare's reason, of his power of moral interpretation', inspiring the questions 'What philosophy of life, what sort of equity?' For Pater, the play demonstrates 'the tyranny of nature and circumstance over human action', where 'the bloodless, impassible temperament does but wait for its opportunity, for the almost accidental coherence of time with place, and place with wishing, to annul its long and patient discipline, and become in a moment the very opposite of that which under ordinary conditions it seemed to be, even to itself'. 'The action of the play', Pater concluded, 'like the action of life itself ... develops in us the conception of ... poetical justice, and the yearning to realise it': 'as the play is full of the peculiarities of Shakespeare's poetry, so in its ethics it is an epitome of Shakespeare's moral judgements'. The *Casebook* on the play, edited by C.K. Stead (Macmillan, 1971) contains useful extracts from early critics, including Samuel Johnson and S.T. Coleridge.

STAGE HISTORY

If critics' response to the play as written literature was, at best, guarded up to the end of the nineteenth century, so too were attitudes to *Measure for Measure* as a piece for the stage. In the Restoration period, the play was twice adapted, once by William Davenant as *The Law Against Lovers* (1662), which interpolated the Beatrice and Benedick plot from *Much Ado About Nothing*, and again by Charles Gildon as *Measure for Measure, or Beauty the Best Advocate* (1700). These adaptations were short lived, however, and during the eighteenth century there were fairly regular productions of Shakespeare's text, with major actors such as John Kemble as the Duke and Mrs Cibber, Mrs Yates and Mrs Siddons as Isabella. Cuts for performance meant the play was increasingly **bowdlerised**, with Juliet's pregnancy only hinted at and the bed-trick so delicately alluded to that it could easily be missed. During the nineteenth century, the play's place in the repertory, never very firm, was further eroded. It was not until the mid twentieth century that *Measure for Measure*'s dramatic potential was fully realised on the stage. Peter Brook's production in 1950 was a landmark, in which the contrasts between the 'religious thought' of the play's ideals and the 'disgusting, stinking world of medieval Vienna' were highlighted. The play's appeal to twentieth-century experience is shown in the number of productions which have updated its setting, often to the late nineteenth- or early twentieth-century Vienna of the pioneer of psychoanalysis, Sigmund Freud.

Measure for Measure's stage history is surveyed in Graham Nicholls's *Measure for Measure: Text and Performance* (Macmillan, 1986). Peter Brook's account of his 1950 production can be found in his *The Empty Space* (1977); Juliet Stevenson and Paula Dionisotti talk about their experiences of playing Isabella in *Clamorous Voices: Shakespeare's Women Today* edited by Carol Rutter (The Women's Press, 1988); and in Roger Smallwood and Russell Jackson's volumes *Players of Shakespeare* (Cambridge University Press), Roger Allam (in volume 3, 1993) and Daniel Massey (in volume 2, 1988) discuss the role of the Duke. Peter Corbin's essay 'Performing *Measure for Measure*' in Nigel Wood, ed., *Measure for Measure* (Open University, 1996) stresses that the play was written for performance and that stage or film productions should be the 'initial critical laboratory, not the study'. Adaptations of the play include *The Law for Lovers* by William Davenant (1662), and, more recently by Howard Brenton, whose version is published in *Three Plays* edited by John Bull (Methuen, 1989). Bertolt Brecht's version of the play, performed in the early 1930s, converted it into *Die Rundköpfe und die*

Spitzkopfe (*Round Heads and Pointed Heads*), a **Marxist** allegory in which the Duke represents capitalism and Angelo Hitler.

TWENTIETH-CENTURY VIEWS

The themes of *Measure for Measure* establish it as a play with particular resonances for the modern period, illustrating the playwright George Bernard Shaw's dictum, in his preface to *Plays Unpleasant* (1898), that in this play Shakespeare is 'ready and willing to start at the twentieth century if only the seventeenth would let him'. It is easy to see why its questioning stance has appealed to the sceptical twentieth century, in which the decline of religion and changing attitudes towards gender and sexuality have heightened its philosophical and dramatic potency. A modern willingness to enjoy its ambiguities and questions has also placed *Measure for Measure* at the centre of the critical and dramatic canon.

C.K. Stead's *Casebook* on the play includes some more recent essays by G. Wilson Knight on '*Measure for Measure* and the Gospels' (in which he argues for a Christian interpretation of the play with the Duke representing a divine principle of justice and mercy) and L.C. Knights on 'The Ambiguity of *Measure for Measure*' (which claims the play's incomplete clarification as a mark of its ethical and philosophical integrity). More recent criticism has tended to highlight Knights's interpretation, stressing questions rather than trying to supply answers: introductory studies by Harriet Hawkins (The Harvester Press, 1987) and Cedric Watts (Penguin, 1986) promote the play's contradictory ethics and moral relativism.

Recent essays written from distinct critical perspectives illuminate *Measure for Measure*. Jonathan Dollimore's 'Transgression and Surveillance in *Measure for Measure*' (in *Political Shakespeare: New Essays in Cultural Materialism* eds Dollimore and Alan Sinfield, Manchester University Press, 1985) stresses a political reading of the play. It dramatises 'an exercise in authoritarian repression', in which the Duke's undercover surveillance of his people and a prevalent Christian morality that stigmatises sex as guilt combine to keep the populace under a sinister form of ideological control. Richard Wilson's 'Prince of Darkness: Foucault's Shakespeare' in Nigel Wood, ed., *Measure for Measure* (Open University, 1996), also stresses authoritarian control in his reading. He adapts the work of the French philosopher-historian, Michel Foucault, and in particular his writings on the rise of the prison as an instrument of social control, to present the Duke's surveillance as a version of the nineteenth-century invention of the Panopticon, a vantage point from which a large area could be surveyed and thereby controlled. It seems that few modern critics have a good word to say for the Duke.

In her book on Shakespeare written from a **feminist** perspective, *Still Harping on Daughters: Women and Drama in the Age of Shakespeare* (Harvester Wheatsheaf, 1983), Lisa Jardine discusses the characterisation of Isabella in the context of Shakespeare's other female roles. She argues that his female characterisation is largely drawn from a range of stereotypes of feminine behaviour, and that while Isabella may seem to resist such stereotypes, her punishment is to be disliked by the play and its audiences. Nicholas Radel also considers the play 'Reading as a Feminist' in Nigel Wood's collection *Measure for Measure*, discussing how Isabella's sexuality is represented and how questions of gender form the basis of the play's argument.

World events	Shakespeare's life	Literary events
1492 Columbus sets sail for America		
		1513 Niccolo Machiavelli, *The Prince* (source)
		1528 Castiglione's *Book of the Courtier*
		1532 Ariosto's *Orlando Furioso*
1534 Henry VIII breaks with Rome		
1556 Archbishop Cranmer burnt at stake		
1558 Elizabeth I accedes to throne		
		1562 Lope de Vega, great Spanish dramatist, born
	1564 (26 April) **William Shakespeare** baptised, Stratford-upon-Avon	
		1565 Giovanni Giraldi Cinthio, *Hecatommithi* (source)
1570 Elizabeth 1 excommunicated by Pope Pius V		
	1576 James Burbage builds the first theatre in England, at Shoreditch	
1577 Francis Drake sets out on voyage round the world		
		1578 George Whetstone, *Promos and Cassandra* (source)
		1580 (c.) Sir Philip Sidney, *An Apologie for Poetrie*
	1582 Shakespeare marries Anne Hathaway	
	1583 Their daughter Susanna born	
1584 Raleigh's sailors land in Virginia		
	1585 Their twins, Hamnet and Judith, born	
1587 Execution of Mary Queen of Scots		
1588 The Spanish Armada defeated		**1588-9** Thomas Kyd, *The Spanish Tragedy*
	late 1580s - early 1590s Probably writes *Henry VI* (Parts I, II & III) and *Richard III*	
		1590 Edmund Spenser, *Faerie Queene* (Books I-III)
1592 Plague in London closes theatres	**1592** Recorded as being a London actor and an 'upstart crow'	
	1592-4 Writes *Comedy of Errors*	
	1594 onwards Writes exclusively for the Lord Chamberlain's Men	

World events	Shakespeare's life	Literary events
	1595 (pre) *Two Gentlemen of Verona, The Taming of the Shrew* and *Love's Labour's Lost* probably written	
	1595 (c.) *Romeo and Juliet*	
1596 English raid on Cadiz	**1596-8** First performance, *The Merchant of Venice*	
	1598-9 Globe Theatre built at Southwark	
	1599 *Henry V*	**1599** Thos Heywood (?), *Edward IV*
	1600 *A Midsummer Night's Dream, Much Ado About Nothing* and *The Merchant of Venice* printed in quartos	
	1600-1 *Hamlet*	**1601** Ben Jonson, *Cynthia's Revels*
	1600-2 *Twelfth Night*	
1603 Death of Queen Elizabeth Tudor; accession of James Stuart; Law passed to demolish brothels in suburbs to prevent spread of Plague	**1603** onwards His company enjoys patronage of James I as the King's Men	
	1604 'Mesur for Mesur' by 'Shaxberd' performed at Palace of Whitehall; *Othello* performed	
1605 Discovery of Guy Fawkes's plot	**1605** First version of *King Lear*	**1605** Cervantes, *Don Quixote de la Mancha*
	1606 *Macbeth*	
	1606-7 *Antony and Cleopatra*	
	1608 The King's Men acquire Blackfriars Theatre for winter performances	
1609 Galileo constructs first astronomical telescope		**1609** Beaumont & Fletcher, *Philastor, or Love Lies-a-Bleeding*
1610 William Harvey discovers circulation of blood		
	1611 *Cymbeline, The Winter's Tale* and *The Tempest* performed	
1612 Last burning of heretics in England		**1612** John Webster, *The White Devil*
	1613 Globe Theatre burns down	
	1616 Death of William Shakespeare	
1618 Thirty Years War begins in Europe		
		1622 Birth of French dramatist Molière
	1623 First folio of Shakespeare's works includes *Measure for Measure* as a comedy	

aside a non-naturalistic dramatic convention allowing characters to voice their thoughts, sometimes addressing the audience directly, without other characters hearing them

blank verse unrhymed iambic pentameter

bowdlerised expurgated, from Dr Thomas Bowdler's *Family Shakespeare* (1818) 'in which those words or expressions are omitted which cannot without propriety be read aloud in a family'

choric in ancient Greek tragedies a chorus was a group of characters who observed the action and commented on it but were not involved or active within it. Choric characters in other types of play tend to be observers rather than participants, and their ironic insights direct the audience's understanding of the events of the drama. Other Shakespearean characters sometimes ascribed a choric function are Enobarbus in *Antony and Cleopatra* and the Fool in *King Lear*

couplet pair of rhymed lines. End-rhyme is common in early Shakespeare plays such as *Richard II* and *The Comedy of Errors* but by the time of *Measure for Measure* it is less frequently employed and therefore worth examining to determine why this form has been chosen

dénouement the final unfolding of a plot

deus ex machina In Greek drama a god was sometimes lowered on to the stage by a piece of machinery, if such an intervention was needed to assist or complete the unfolding of the plot. The term is used to describe any unexpected or improbable intervention to resolve the action

dramatic irony a commonly used device by which the audience possesses more information about events than the characters themselves. In comedy this knowledge is often a source of humour

feminist criticism a way of reading literature by stressing the role of gender in the text, its production and its reception

First Folio the first collected edition of Shakespeare's plays, published posthumously in 1623. The word 'folio' refers to the large size of the book made from sheets of paper with only one fold

gnomic verse containing maxims of popular wisdom, short, impressive statements of general truths

hubris the complacent self-confidence that causes a tragic hero to ignore the laws and warnings of the gods and therefore defy them to bring about his or her downfall

hyperbole a figure of speech which gives emphasis through exaggeration

iambic pentameter an iamb is a metrical foot consisting of a weak stress followed by a strong stress, ti-tum. There are five of these in a line of iambic pentameter

Machiavellian adjective derived from Renaissance perceptions of the works of Florentine writer Niccolo Machiavelli (1469–1527), who wrote a book of political advice to rulers called *The Prince* (1513). In this work he recommended preserving power by manipulating the populace. *The Prince* contains one particular story which may be of relevance to *Measure for Measure*. It tells how the duke Cesare Borgia took over a state in which the law had become disregarded, so he gave absolute powers to a deputy to reinstate good government. This the deputy achieved through harsh and cruel enforcement of the law and was unpopular with the people. Then Borgia returned and, in order to win the newly subdued people over to him, he wanted to demonstrate that the repressive laws had come not from him but from the deputy. He arranged for the deputy's dissected body to be displayed in the central square. 'The ferocity of this scene', writes Machiavelli, 'left the people at once stunned and satisfied'

malapropism mistaken and muddled use of long words: so called after Mrs Malaprop in Sheridan's play *The Rivals* (1775) who constantly utters nonsense in her attempts to sound learned. As well as in *Measure for Measure,* Shakespeare uses the device to characterise the comic constable Dogberry in *Much Ado About Nothing*

Marxist criticism criticism that considers literature in relation to its capacity to reflect the struggle between the classes, and the economic conditions which, according to Karl Marx (1818–83) and Friedrich Engels (1820–95), lie at the basis of man's intellectual and social evolution

metaphor a comparison between two things or ideas, made by fusing them together: one thing is described as being another thing, thus carrying over its associations: e.g. 'The needful bits and curbs to headstrong weeds' (I.3.20)

Method a technique of acting based on the theories of Russian actor and director Konstantin Stanislavsky (1863–1938) in which ideas about the inner motivations and psychology of a character are the basis of the performance

peripeteia in comedy, a sudden change in events for the better

personification a figure of speech in which things or abstract ideas are treated as if they were human beings, with human attributes and feelings

quarto book size in which the paper is folded four times

simile a figure of speech in which something is said to be 'like' or 'as' another thing

soliloquy (from the Latin 'to speak alone') dramatic convention which allows a character in a play to speak directly to the audience as if thinking aloud about motives, feelings and decisions

syntax the arrangement of words in a particular form and order so as to achieve meaning

verisimilitude likeness to reality or truth

Author of this note

Emma Smith is a Fellow in English Literature at New Hall, Cambridge. Her teaching and research interests are in the drama of Shakespeare and his contemporaries. She was born in Leeds and educated at Somerville College, Oxford.

Notes

NOTES

NOTES

Notes

NOTES

Notes

NOTES

ADVANCED LEVEL TITLES

York Notes Advanced (£3.99 each)

Margaret Atwood
The Handmaid's Tale

Jane Austen
Mansfield Park

Jane Austen
Persuasion

Jane Austen
Pride and Prejudice

Alan Bennett
Talking Heads

William Blake
Songs of Innocence and of Experience

Charlotte Brontë
Jane Eyre

Emily Brontë
Wuthering Heights

Geoffrey Chaucer
The Franklin's Tale

Geoffrey Chaucer
General Prologue to the Canterbury Tales

Geoffrey Chaucer
The Wife of Bath's Prologue and Tale

Joseph Conrad
Heart of Darkness

Charles Dickens
Great Expectations

John Donne
Selected Poems

George Eliot
The Mill on the Floss

F. Scott Fitzgerald
The Great Gatsby

E.M. Forster
A Passage to India

Brian Friel
Translations

Thomas Hardy
The Mayor of Casterbridge

Thomas Hardy
Tess of the d'Urbervilles

Seamus Heaney
Selected Poems from Opened Ground

Nathaniel Hawthorne
The Scarlet Letter

James Joyce
Dubliners

John Keats
Selected Poems

Christopher Marlowe
Doctor Faustus

Arthur Miller
Death of a Salesman

Toni Morrison
Beloved

William Shakespeare
Antony and Cleopatra

William Shakespeare
As You Like It

William Shakespeare
Hamlet

William Shakespeare
King Lear

William Shakespeare
Measure for Measure

William Shakespeare
The Merchant of Venice

William Shakespeare
Much Ado About Nothing

William Shakespeare
Othello

William Shakespeare
Romeo and Juliet

William Shakespeare
The Tempest

William Shakespeare
The Winter's Tale

Mary Shelley
Frankenstein

Alice Walker
The Color Purple

Oscar Wilde
The Importance of Being Earnest

Tennessee Williams
A Streetcar Named Desire

John Webster
The Duchess of Malfi

W.B. Yeats
Selected Poems

GCSE and equivalent levels (£3.50 each)

Maya Angelou
I Know Why the Caged Bird Sings

Jane Austen
Pride and Prejudice

Alan Ayckbourn
Absent Friends

Elizabeth Barrett Browning
Selected Poems

Robert Bolt
A Man for All Seasons

Harold Brighouse
Hobson's Choice

Charlotte Brontë
Jane Eyre

Emily Brontë
Wuthering Heights

Shelagh Delaney
A Taste of Honey

Charles Dickens
David Copperfield

Charles Dickens
Great Expectations

Charles Dickens
Hard Times

Charles Dickens
Oliver Twist

Roddy Doyle
Paddy Clarke Ha Ha Ha

George Eliot
Silas Marner

George Eliot
The Mill on the Floss

William Golding
Lord of the Flies

Oliver Goldsmith
She Stoops To Conquer

Willis Hall
The Long and the Short and the Tall

Thomas Hardy
Far from the Madding Crowd

Thomas Hardy
The Mayor of Casterbridge

Thomas Hardy
Tess of the d'Urbervilles

Thomas Hardy
The Withered Arm and other Wessex Tales

L.P. Hartley
The Go-Between

Seamus Heaney
Selected Poems

Susan Hill
I'm the King of the Castle

Barry Hines
A Kestrel for a Knave

Louise Lawrence
Children of the Dust

Harper Lee
To Kill a Mockingbird

Laurie Lee
Cider with Rosie

Arthur Miller
The Crucible

Arthur Miller
A View from the Bridge

Robert O'Brien
Z for Zachariah

Frank O'Connor
My Oedipus Complex and other stories

George Orwell
Animal Farm

J.B. Priestley
An Inspector Calls

Willy Russell
Educating Rita

Willy Russell
Our Day Out

J.D. Salinger
The Catcher in the Rye

William Shakespeare
Henry IV Part 1

William Shakespeare
Henry V

William Shakespeare
Julius Caesar

William Shakespeare
Macbeth

William Shakespeare
The Merchant of Venice

William Shakespeare
A Midsummer Night's Dream

William Shakespeare
Much Ado About Nothing

William Shakespeare
Romeo and Juliet

William Shakespeare
The Tempest

William Shakespeare
Twelfth Night

George Bernard Shaw
Pygmalion

Mary Shelley
Frankenstein

R.C. Sherriff
Journey's End

Rukshana Smith
Salt on the snow

John Steinbeck
Of Mice and Men

Robert Louis Stevenson
Dr Jekyll and Mr Hyde

Jonathan Swift
Gulliver's Travels

Robert Swindells
Daz 4 Zoe

Mildred D. Taylor
Roll of Thunder, Hear My Cry

Mark Twain
Huckleberry Finn

James Watson
Talking in Whispers

William Wordsworth
Selected Poems

A Choice of Poets

Mystery Stories of the Nineteenth Century including The Signalman

Nineteenth Century Short Stories

Poetry of the First World War

Six Women Poets

Chinua Achebe
Things Fall Apart

Edward Albee
Who's Afraid of Virginia Woolf?

Margaret Atwood
Cat's Eye

Jane Austen
Emma

Jane Austen
Northanger Abbey

Jane Austen
Sense and Sensibility

Samuel Beckett
Waiting for Godot

Robert Browning
Selected Poems

Robert Burns
Selected Poems

Angela Carter
Nights at the Circus

Geoffrey Chaucer
The Merchant's Tale

Geoffrey Chaucer
The Miller's Tale

Geoffrey Chaucer
The Nun's Priest's Tale

Samuel Taylor Coleridge
Selected Poems

Daniel Defoe
Moll Flanders

Daniel Defoe
Robinson Crusoe

Charles Dickens
Bleak House

Charles Dickens
Hard Times

Emily Dickinson
Selected Poems

Carol Ann Duffy
Selected Poems

George Eliot
Middlemarch

T.S. Eliot
The Waste Land

T.S. Eliot
Selected Poems

Henry Fielding
Joseph Andrews

E.M. Forster
Howards End

John Fowles
The French Lieutenant's Woman

Robert Frost
Selected Poems

Elizabeth Gaskell
North and South

Stella Gibbons
Cold Comfort Farm

Graham Greene
Brighton Rock

Thomas Hardy
Jude the Obscure

Thomas Hardy
Selected Poems

Joseph Heller
Catch-22

Homer
The Iliad

Homer
The Odyssey

Gerard Manley Hopkins
Selected Poems

Aldous Huxley
Brave New World

Kazuo Ishiguro
The Remains of the Day

Ben Jonson
The Alchemist

Ben Jonson
Volpone

James Joyce
A Portrait of the Artist as a Young Man

Philip Larkin
Selected Poems

D.H. Lawrence
The Rainbow

D.H. Lawrence
Selected Stories

D.H. Lawrence
Sons and Lovers

D.H. Lawrence
Women in Love

John Milton
Paradise Lost Bks I & II

John Milton
Paradise Lost Bks IV & IX

Thomas More
Utopia

Sean O'Casey
Juno and the Paycock

George Orwell
Nineteen Eighty-four

John Osborne
Look Back in Anger

Wilfred Owen
Selected Poems

Sylvia Plath
Selected Poems

Alexander Pope
Rape of the Lock and other poems

Ruth Prawer Jhabvala
Heat and Dust

Jean Rhys
Wide Sargasso Sea

William Shakespeare
As You Like It

William Shakespeare
Coriolanus

William Shakespeare
Henry IV Pt 1

William Shakespeare
Henry V

William Shakespeare
Julius Caesar

William Shakespeare
Macbeth

William Shakespeare
Measure for Measure

William Shakespeare
A Midsummer Night's Dream

William Shakespeare
Richard II

William Shakespeare
Richard III

William Shakespeare
Sonnets

William Shakespeare
The Taming of the Shrew

William Shakespeare
Twelfth Night

William Shakespeare
The Winter's Tale

George Bernard Shaw
Arms and the Man

George Bernard Shaw
Saint Joan

Muriel Spark
The Prime of Miss Jean Brodie

John Steinbeck
The Grapes of Wrath

John Steinbeck
The Pearl

Tom Stoppard
Arcadia

Tom Stoppard
Rosencrantz and Guildenstern are Dead

Jonathan Swift
Gulliver's Travels and The Modest Proposal

Alfred, Lord Tennyson
Selected Poems

W.M. Thackeray
Vanity Fair

Virgil
The Aeneid

Edith Wharton
The Age of Innocence

Tennessee Williams
Cat on a Hot Tin Roof

Tennessee Williams
The Glass Menagerie

Virginia Woolf
Mrs Dalloway

Virginia Woolf
To the Lighthouse

William Wordsworth
Selected Poems

Metaphysical Poets

York Notes – the Ultimate Literature Guides

York Notes are recognised as the best literature study guides.
If you have enjoyed using this book and have found it useful, you
can now order others directly from us – simply follow the ordering
instructions below.

HOW TO ORDER

Decide which title(s) you require and then order in one of the following
ways:

Booksellers
All titles available from good bookstores.

By post
List the title(s) you require in the space provided overleaf,
select your method of payment, complete your name and
address details and return your completed order form and
payment to:
> *Addison Wesley Longman Ltd*
> *PO BOX 88*
> *Harlow*
> *Essex CM19 5SR*

By phone
Call our Customer Information Centre on 01279 623923 to
place your order, quoting mail number: HEYN1.

By fax
Complete the order form overleaf, ensuring you fill in your
name and address details and method of payment, and fax it
to us on 01279 414130.

By e-mail
E-mail your order to us on awlhe.orders@awl.co.uk listing
title(s) and quantity required and providing full name and
address details as requested overleaf. Please quote mail
number: HEYN1. Please do not send credit card details by
e-mail.

York Notes Order Form

Titles required:

Quantity	Title/ISBN	Price

Sub total _____

Please add £2.50 postage & packing _____

(P & P is free for orders over £50) _____

Total _____

Mail no: HEYN1

Your Name _____

Your Address _____

_____

Postcode _____ Telephone _____

Method of payment

☐ I enclose a cheque or a P/O for £_____ made payable to Addison Wesley Longman Ltd

☐ Please charge my Visa/Access/AMEX/Diners Club card
Number _____ Expiry Date _____
Signature _____ Date _____

(please ensure that the address given above is the same as for your credit card)

Prices and other details are correct at time of going to press but may change without notice. All orders are subject to status.

☐ *Please tick this box if you would like a complete listing of Longman Study Guides (suitable for GCSE and A-level students)*

York Press

Longman

Addison
Wesley
Longman